"A masterful project manager and one of the best educators in the project management discipline, Robin Hornby does an excellent job in *A Concise Guide to Project Collaboration*. The guide walks the reader through the business lifecycle, focusing clearly on the business interest and the client's share of responsibilities. At each stage the guide defines the collaborative steps as part of a clear project plan, emphasizing critical communications, agreements, and accountabilities. The approach includes assessing and documenting project successes, and a final analysis 'Did we Benefit?'. Hornby's methods have saved significant dollars for companies I have worked for. This guide will further strengthen our ability to deliver professional projects to our customers."

James R. Wickson, *Vice President, Esri Canada*

"In *A Concise Guide to Project Collaboration*, Robin Hornby culminates decades of experience successfully delivering programs and projects. He takes a holistic project delivery perspective and goes beyond the core capabilities and practices of project management to provide frameworks and guidance for the 'Delivery Organization'. Hornby describes this as a high performing collaborative, business-oriented environment, and a frequently overlooked component of success. This is a must-read for executives, sponsors, leaders, and business stakeholders who are accountable for project outcomes and business benefits, as well as their supporting consulting firms and service providers."

Jackie Poeckens, *Partner, Sia Partners*

"Robin Hornby's *A Concise Guide to Project Collaboration* is a valuable read for managers and employees collaborating with the project provider to achieve project success. The guide is clearly written, and the concepts are enhanced with practical visuals and templates. I appreciated the strong emphasis on project accountability, quality, risks, and resources."

Kam Jugdev, *Professor, Project Management and Strategy, Athabasca University*

"If you are one of those many project managers who have been frustrated by the lack of direction, support, and accountability from the Board, Executive and Business Management, Hornby's focus in *A Concise Guide to Project Collaboration* will help you navigate your way to a successful outcome."

John Thorp, *Author of* The Information Paradox,
*Fujitsu Consulting Fellow, Fellow of The Innovation
Value Institute, and the Institute for
Digital Transformation*

"*A Concise Guide to Project Collaboration* draws upon Robin Hornby's vast experience and delivers a ground-breaking, easy to understand, actionable resource for collaborative and successful delivery of complex projects. This guide is a tremendous resource for all business leaders and project professionals who want to know what to do, and how to do it."

Russ Hall, *former President, Intergraph Canada*

A Concise Guide to Project Collaboration

Easy to read and act on immediately, this concise guide shows how organizations can work more effectively with in-house or contracted project managers and their teams, using specific collaborative techniques to improve success rates, reduce project costs, and enable organizations to benefit from common-sense, cost-effective project management approaches that work.

Using a clear structure and accessible style, the book demonstrates how:

- Managers can create an organizational environment more naturally adapted for project work and recognition of business priorities;
- Barriers to project work can be removed so project managers can focus on resolving real project problems;
- Specific collaborative project management methods engaging business owners, users, and technical teams can be illuminated and implemented;
- Projects can fit within an architecture that aligns with business needs using models and workflow designs; and
- Standardized delivery management can unify in-house and vendor teams to create a uniform and predictable owner experience.

The book is aimed at managers and executives (both IT and users) in corporations and vendor firms who are engaged in delivering projects. The book will also be invaluable to any project manager or senior practitioner who is interested in a business-oriented, unified, and collaborative approach to project management.

Robin Hornby worked in Information Technology for over 40 years, rising from a technical role to project and delivery management. He taught project management at Mount Royal University for 12 years and maintained a consulting practice. He has authored four books and pioneered many of the delivery practices described in this guide.

A Concise Guide to Project Collaboration
Building a Delivery Organization

Robin Hornby

Routledge
Taylor & Francis Group

LONDON AND NEW YORK

First published 2023
by Routledge
4 Park Square, Milton Park, Abingdon, Oxon OX14 4RN

and by Routledge
605 Third Avenue, New York, NY 10158

Routledge is an imprint of the Taylor & Francis Group, an informa business

© 2023 Robin Hornby

British Library Cataloguing-in-Publication Data
A catalogue record for this book is available from the British Library

Library of Congress Cataloging-in-Publication Data
Names: Hornby, Robin, 1945– author.
Title: A concise guide to project collaboration : building a delivery organization / Robin Hornby.
Description: New York, NY : Routledge, 2023. | Includes bibliographical references and index.
Identifiers: LCCN 2022054917 (print) | LCCN 2022054918 (ebook) | ISBN 9781032435459 (hardback) | ISBN 9781032440262 (paperback) | ISBN 9781003370031 (ebook)
Subjects: LCSH: Project management. | Business planning. | Organizational change.
Classification: LCC HD69.P75 H67286 2023 (print) | LCC HD69.P75 (ebook) | DDC 658.4/04—dc23
LC record available at https://lccn.loc.gov/2022054917
LC ebook record available at https://lccn.loc.gov/2022054918

ISBN: 978-1-032-43545-9 (hbk)
ISBN: 978-1-032-44026-2 (pbk)
ISBN: 978-1-003-37003-1 (ebk)

DOI: 10.4324/9781003370031

Typeset in Times
by Apex CoVantage, LLC

Contents

Foreword

Think back to some of the projects you have been involved in, as a senior corporate stakeholder, a vendor manager, or a project manager. A few were probably rated as successful, a few didn't work out, and the majority came out as mediocre – they mostly achieved what was required but took longer and cost more. Perhaps, you may be thinking, with better project management, results could have been improved, and the experience could have been less painful.

It is always tempting to pin blame on the project manager when things go awry, that is, after all, where the responsibility for success was allocated. Some blame may well be deserved, but my observation over the years suggests the organization itself places so many obstacles in the project manager's way that exceptional skills are often required for achievement.

The last few decades have seen a tremendous and welcome emphasis on the methods and techniques of project management and the training of project managers. And yet the environment in which projects take place also has significant influence on the efficiency of the project and even the likelihood of it achieving its objectives. Almost without exception, corporate managers and employees believe they have little obligation toward the success of a project they may be involved in. They see that as the project manager's job. Yet this is in contradiction to other corporate endeavors, where it is now commonplace for employees to be educated on human resources policies and procedures, likewise for quality, safety, ethics, corporate mission, public relations, and possibly more. Surely the time has now come to ensure the senior people and managers in our organizations know how to collaborate to get the job done when a project comes their way. I call this the Delivery Organization.

Robin Hornby worked in Information Technology for over 40 years, taught project management at Mount Royal University for 12 years, and maintained a consulting practice. He pioneered many of the delivery practices described in this guide.

Introduction

Collaboration makes project work go easier. Striving to meet the owner's need for better business control of the project also leads to better project outcomes. Then why are both requirements so poorly served by current project management standards, methodology, and training? A provider who is motivated to understand and report business information will naturally want to adopt a collaborative approach with the owner. An owner who is discouraged from project participation by poor integration also needs a defined collaborative framework. The resolution of these needs creates an organization primed for delivery – a Delivery Organization.

The book is not about project management or development methodology. You'll find plenty of those already on the (e)shelves. My intent is to assemble a guide and usage templates to show why and how the owner and provider can work collaboratively through the stages of project delivery. Some elements of project management will be recognized, but I do not explicate upon conventional project management knowledge. Nor is my interpretation of collaboration referring to the common circumstance of a project manager working collaboratively with the team. Such an approach just requires the common-sense need to consult prior to decision-making, to listen to ideas, to ensure tasks are assigned with care and amended on the basis of feedback, that results are valued, and everyone is treated respectfully. Neither am I referring to non-hierarchical self-directed teams which may or may not be collaborative but in most cases are no way to run a project. All these ideas are discussed elsewhere in the literature.

The goal of the Delivery Organization (or DO for short) is to ensure projects proceed unencumbered by needless obstacles. A secondary intent is to provide a unified business lifecycle allowing consistent business management, independent of the decision to use an in-house provider or a vendor. The required actions cost little to perform, even less to maintain, and the payback is large for any organization which runs more than a project or two each year. There are two themes. The first is the introduction of

DOI: 10.4324/9781003370031-1

collaboration to improve delivery performance. The second is an increased focus on the *business management* of projects to match the owner's over-riding interest and to encourage attention to business priorities and relevant reporting from the provider. This guide, therefore, is aimed at general managers and executives who wish to build an environment in which projects thrive, not struggle.

When projects fail, meaning they do not deliver the required result within the approved cost and schedule, the project manager takes the blame. This is as it should be because the project manager is accountable for the success of the project. But sometimes this is not quite fair. Sometimes the project manager is expected not just to deliver the project but also to deal with anomalies in the environment. A good, experienced project manager might be able to overcome these difficulties, and most do; the drawbacks are project risks and costs higher than they need be, and too few good and experienced project managers to go around.

So, the hypothesis I promote is an organizational environment *inherently* favorable to planning and executing projects. The new environment will encourage or even mandate the behavior required by managers and executives. After a period, a transformed corporate culture will emerge that might remove much of the grind from project operations and maybe even make some of it a pleasure! Many of the internal sources of project risk will also be removed. This is not to be confused with a discretionary toolkit offered to project managers. Project toolkits are usually aimed at helping project managers with different approaches and techniques, eschewing a 'one-size-fits-all'. That is not what I am discussing. What is proposed is a certainty of the *operating environment*, a clear expectation for all stakeholders, always recognizable, and always compatible. There is no choice to be made and no chance of being wrong.

Although the analogy is imperfect, and in some quarters the example is controversial, the corporate approach to quality over the last few decades provides an illustration of how project work could be embedded within the corporate environment. Initially, project managers who understood the importance of quality principles specified their own quality procedures and designed a supportive project structure. They had to sell the resulting increase in cost. This was burdensome and sometimes futile as success with quality initiatives is hard to achieve without top-down executive commitment. Eventually, quality-conscious organizations realized that top-down corporate-wide implementations such as ISO9000, Total Quality Management (TQM), or Six Sigma were necessary if conformity was the goal. Quality was not an option and in time became embedded in the culture.

The comparison of delivery with quality has some exceptions which are important to highlight. First, though proponents argue long-term costs are reduced, there can be no doubt quality initiatives add to the work, add to the management, and therefore add to project cost. This is not analogous to the DO. In most cases, the project will incur similar costs in any event, probably inflated because of natural friction. Any increase in management cost from explicitly adding the DO is modest. Second, guarantees of prescribed quality work flounder when work must be contracted out. How can TQM or Six Sigma be assured? Admittedly, ISO9000 is structured to demand subcontracting organizations must also be fully certified for the standard to be met, but it is tedious and expensive. On the other hand, a uniform DO is beneficial for both the owner and the provider. They know exactly the environment they are going to work in, and there is no significant cost.

Already some terminology is being used to delineate the subject matter. A glossary is included to provide a useful lookup facility, but here are the terms now being used:

- The Owner of the Project: The generic name for the sponsoring organization and beneficiary of the project. It includes the individual role of project sponsor whose responsibility is funding and the harvesting of business benefit, and the role of a business team who assists with the project. When the project is contracted, the owner is also referred to as the client.
- The Provider of the Project: The generic name for the organization providing the technical team and delivering the project according to scope, budget, and schedule. If the provider is part of the owner organization, they may be termed the in-house provider. If the provider is contracted, they may be referred to as the vendor.
- The Delivery Organization (DO): A collective term for both the owner and the provider who have adopted the themes of collaboration and business management of projects and are working together.

The guide touches on the emerging topic of 'project business management' though it's a term I generally avoid as the terminology is too fluid. Roughly three different but related meanings can be found in current project literature on the subject. Business management in the project context can mean:

- Commercial Project Management: Executing projects under contract and managing the business conditions to include the vendor's benefit.
- Business Alignment: Managing projects with a priority to business outcomes, under business control, and therefore reconciling the business interests of owner and vendor (if engaged). This is the guide's primary perspective.
- Project Management as a Business Function: Managing the business following project management principles and implementing a Project Management Office (PMO) to drive those processes into the business. As a believer in project management, I appreciate the intent of this philosophy,

but I think it's more useful to invert this and add business principles to project management, thus treating business as a knowledge area of project management. The PMO then clearly functions as a support and standard-bearer for projects, but with an understanding of business.

I don't want to entangle the reader in these potentially confusing complications, although it's impossible to discuss my topic without these concepts entering in. I attempt to keep my language as plain as possible, to be easily read by a non-specialist and immediately actionable. The guide provides specific instruction supported by simple diagrams to explain complex issues and illustrate their solution. It unifies in-house and vendor business management and adopts an organization-centric view to show how individual projects can be delivered more effectively with owner/provider collaboration. The owner is given business control, and the provider retains project control. This is a Delivery Organization aligned with the business.

In the opening chapter of this guide, I explore organizational issues in detail, with an eye on the most suitable guarantor and curator of the new DO. This is followed by a set of models which help the reader understand how project architecture can accommodate the owner's need for business management, how to leverage the dynamics of the owner/provider relationship, and how to counter the causes of owner/provider disengagement.

An analysis of these models defines the foundation of a Delivery Organization which reduces, if not eliminates, recurring frictions and impediments encountered by projects. These designs are expanded into 22 techniques drawn from both administrative practice and those professional practices easily adapted for collaboration between owner and provider. Everyone agrees with the exhortations to collaborate, frequently heard from organizational experts, but collaboration in complex project work needs specific direction to make success likely. This guide explains what to do and how to implement it.

I have supplied references to assist the reader who may be seeking more information on project or delivery management specifics. These include details on implementing models and techniques, templates for forms, checklists, document specifications, and example process descriptions. I have included a reference at the end of the chapter where first cited, but rather than repeating it every time such information might be of interest (which could be most chapters), the reference section has been expanded with a brief description of the information it contains, allowing the reader to judge its relevance.

Robin Hornby
Calgary 2022

1 The Organization and the Project

Project work does not fit well with most organizations. This is primarily because their goals are different. A typical organization is established to maintain repetitive activities designed to repeatedly achieve a complex outcome and aims to resource a stable workplace in perpetuity. This might be building a car or completing a financial trade. These repeatable activities are usually monitored using monthly targets. Organizational units tend to be highly specialized and preoccupied with efficiency. A management hierarchy is inevitable and works well for functional coordination and decision-making. However, managers become possessive of their staff and may be reluctant to assign resources to work on improvements that require collaboration with other units.

A project, on the other hand, must achieve the unique defined result and then finish. Resources are assembled and then disbanded at the end of the project. Projects are always competing for resources, aiming to minimize management overhead, and trying to stay nimble. Decisions focus on delivering a scope of work compliant with schedule, quality, and cost, with less attention to operational efficiency. Targets are based on completing interim deliverables or achieving milestones defined as stepping stones to the final result.

This chapter discusses the problems arising from this incompatibility and recent management innovations aiming to fix the disconnect and resolve related issues.

The Matrix Adaptation

The first challenge arises from superimposing a project objective on the neat and tidy functional organization of the typical company. If the objective is a new corporate system, the project manager (PM) is going to need team resources from the Information Technology (IT) group and, as an example,

DOI: 10.4324/9781003370031-2

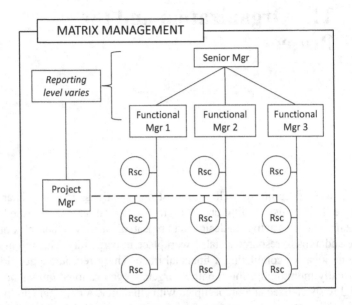

Figure 1.1 Matrix management

from Accounting, Production, and Purchasing. And these people already have a full-time job and a boss!

The fix for this dilemma is to implement some version of matrix management, like Figure 1.1.

Depending upon the relative power of the PM, this arrangement is referred to as either a strong or a weak matrix. The most explicit way to set up a strong matrix is to report the PM to the executive level. A weak matrix would report the PM to a level equal to the functional managers required to lend resources to the project. There are other ways to organize project work, but the matrix is by far the most common despite the weaknesses inherent in the 'two bosses' scenario. Although the matrix management approach addresses many of the problems of superimposing a project on a functional organization and can be successful with the right PM, one shouldn't rely on this approach to completely resolve the more fundamental issues, summarized as follows:

Projects Don't Fit in the Organization

- Projects are Disruptive. In fact, they are occasionally designed to be disruptive to both the hierarchy and the established pattern of repetitive activity. Sometimes, because of expected negative changes to their position, staff provide only reluctant cooperation and lack motivation.

- Unfamiliar Skills. A project also demands skills and processes with which functional staff and their managers may not be familiar. Often, the desirable processes are not clearly perceived and therefore executed poorly or not at all. This uncertainty often extends to the nature of the project role itself and the responsibilities associated with it, some of which come as a surprise. Examples of this are as follows: the need to estimate work effort needed for a project task, their own future availability, the need for quality control, the expectation for review and approval, and even the need to provide intelligible status. This is complicated by having to deal with a PM whose role and interests they may not be sympathetic with.
- Unfamiliar Team. Trying to build a cohesive team under these circumstances is difficult and will be complicated by the probability many team members will not have worked closely together before and do not know each other.

This illustrates the challenges of developing a project culture within a typical organization and the complications the PM is expected to deal with. This, of course, is in addition to the 'normal' problems within the scope of the project itself which are discussed in standard project management texts.

Organizational Innovations

I have encountered four organizational innovations during my experiences as PM, each one of which can be instrumental in surmounting some of the problems I have just described and each of which could contribute to the management accountability needed to implement a Delivery Organization. This role I will christen as the DO Curator and will explain more later.

Chief Information Officer (CIO)

In the early days of dealing with computer systems, often referred to as Data Processing (DP), corporations found it quite natural to embed the DP function within the Finance Department which were typically the first to exploit computerization. Paradoxically, because of this unity and the absence of cross-department coordination requirements, many of the problems I have noted did not exist. Of course, when the need for computer systems became corporate-wide, Finance ownership of DP became unworkable, and a function known as Computer Services or similar was evolved and usually lumped within the catch-all department of Corporate Services.

Eventually, as communications and office technologies became digital and computer systems themselves participated in networks, these elements were integrated into a function now universally known as Information Technology (IT). The next step, which is largely where we are now, was to recognize IT as a significant and strategic element in how the organization does business and thus a major determinant of its success. The head of IT, now known as the CIO, occupies an executive position and commands large budgets. In addition to managing a technology department and ensuring the technology needs of the entire organization are met, the CIO is also charged with developing and maintaining strategic plans based on generating and exploiting information, and enabling this through the future corporate deployment of IT. No small job.

As a promoter of IT solutions, the CIO is in a very powerful position to ensure delivery follows good project practices and exists within a good supporting framework. The ability to do this depends upon the capability of project management within the department, and the willingness and knowledge of the system owners outside the IT department to fulfil their role. This latter point is crucial, because CIO authority is typically limited to the provider organization.

The Project Management Office (PMO)

The idea of a Project Management Office (PMO) is a bit old to be an innovation but is by no means universally implemented. It is clearly on the provider side of the equation, would report to the IT head or the CIO, and is tasked with a variety of responsibilities of concern to all projects. (There is another version of the PMO which is project-specific and usually acts as an administrative arm of the PM on larger projects.) Some PMO duties are as follows:

Duties of a Departmental PMO

- Specifying project standards
- Policing the completion and approval of key project documents
- Assessing project status
- Completing project risk analyses and audits
- Recruiting, developing, assigning, and assessing PMs
- Offering advice and guidance to PMs
- Project administration
- Developing project management tools, techniques, processes, and procedures
- Undertaking independent project post-mortems and identifying the lessons learned

There is great variance in the PMO mandate; the previous list is by no means comprehensive but could also overstate the role in some companies. The major distinction is between a *passive* and an *active* PMO which determines whether the PMO mandate is primarily supportive or directive.

A PMO is usually staffed and managed by veteran PMs and is undoubtedly an asset when it comes to creating an environment for project success. Much depends on how adept the PMO is in presenting itself as a friend of projects and not as an authoritarian policeman. Again, the greatest difficulty I see when it comes to establishing a pro-project culture is an unbalanced alignment with the provider role and a neglect of the owner role. That role is often misunderstood, its importance underestimated, and viewed too much from a distance.

Delivery Management (DM)

A delivery manager is a senior-level individual who embodies many of the characteristics of a PMO. The main distinctions of the delivery manager are (1) clearly stands accountable for the project deliveries by the department and therefore must act as a functional manager for the PMs, (2) understands and articulates the business dimension of projects, monitoring and reporting on those aspects to executive, and (3) must also play a strong role in validating deliverability and completing due diligence on the owner's project proposals *before* they are accepted into project operations. This latter responsibility is a prerequisite to fulfil the first two responsibilities and provides a point of project continuity during feasibility work, as quite often no PM has been appointed. And although DM is primarily a provider role, this front-end engagement puts the delivery manager in direct touch with owner interests (certainly budget) and other go/no-go concerns.

This role originated in the project vendor community and their need to take a specialized interest in the business management of projects, specific contractual obligations, risk, and gross margin. Suitably adapted, its full relevance to companies with in-house providers is still gaining appreciation.

The evolution of the DM role accelerates as the vendor grows from a decentralized to a centralized structure, or as the requirement for formal delivery processes becomes evident. The reporting structure for vendor PMs then changes from the conventional professional services manager to the specialized delivery manager. The DM becomes directly responsible for the project management function and building and maintaining this capability.

In smaller vendors, or those with a decentralized structure, it might be more usual to leave the personnel management and responsibility for developing PMs with the professional services managers but delegate the delivery oversight role to a DM. This produces a matrixed structure where the

PM has two bosses (never mind the contractual 'boss' at the client) and might be considered inferior to establishing a strong DM team. The weakest solution would be no DM structure at all, so both project delivery and personnel management responsibilities belong to the professional services manager.

Management costs become a factor when the vendor migrates to specialized delivery management, which tends to favor the flexibility of the matrixed DM model. Using the matrix, one DM can oversee many projects, even over many locations, being free of responsibility for personnel management of PMs. This model adapts quite well to in-house providers.

Several scenarios will shape ways in which a client delivery manager relates to a vendor project. Most likely, both vendor and client will appoint their respective PMs who, ideally, will operate within our proposed DO to carry out the work of the project. Under this circumstance, both DMs would monitor the project according to their normal criteria and each would act as the first point of escalation for project issues. Note the sponsor then becomes further removed as an escalation point and would represent higher-level interests.

The Value Management Office (VMO)

The concept of a Value Management Office (VMO) emerged primarily to ensure corporate investment in IT is being managed in a rational manner, having regard to project risk, potential return on investment (benefits), and amount of capital required. The encouraging aspect of a VMO is the focus on elements within the owner or sponsor's domain of interest and control. This view, however, is solely from the business benefit perspective, with little or no attention to supporting the owner's responsibility during the delivery process. There are circumstances, however, when this view might be broadened. Many CIOs employ a senior position often known as a customer service or liaison manager. Their responsibilities include liaison between owner and provider on defined issues, owner awareness and marketing of IT services and capabilities, and reporting of owner needs and wants to IT. Folding this position into a VMO makes the result look very compatible as a home for the DO.

The VMO might be seen as operating on behalf of an IT strategy committee, a capital planning committee, or similar. This standing committee of department representatives is primarily concerned with identification, validation, and prioritization of IT project proposals. Inevitably, the committee is almost always chaired by the CIO which tends to position project proposals within the provider's frame and not the owners. It also seems to perpetuate the old condescending power structure where the IT department was always instrumental in getting a project off the ground. Countering this bias suggests keeping the VMO independent of the CIO, conceiving the VMO as a mirror image of the PMO. This implies reporting the VMO to the committee or the CEO, though both options are seen to be managerially inefficient. If the VMO reverts to reporting within the IT department or even within the PMO, this might compromise the VMO as a friend, proponent, and influencer of department project owners. Regardless, the challenge with the promising VMO/Customer Services arrangement as a home for the Delivery Organization Curator (DOC) is to achieve management efficiency while maintaining the visible objectivity of a manager who will have obligations to both provider and owner.

2 A Reference Framework for Collaboration

This chapter introduces six models to help understand the context and the options for the Delivery Organization. The first model is an architecture for the project world that includes a business perspective. This architectural view includes the three derivative domains: business management, project management, and project work. This naturally expands into the second model, the business lifecycle, and additional models for the project management functions and the project lifecycle. The fifth model illustrates the critical dynamic provided by a proper understanding of the owner/provider balance. And the sixth and final model is the silo effect and how its proper recognition can assist with project integration.

Project Architecture

Our architectural model highlights the three domains of the project and emphasizes their distinction. This has been absent from traditional project frameworks, and the different domains have consequently been muddled together.

The model drawn in Figure 2.1, which recognizes both in-house and vendor providers, requires selection of alternative paths during project materialization. The materialization stage for the owner and the vendor (if engaged) is shown as converging into the collaborative common delivery stages.

The three domains are as follows:

(1) Business Management. This is, or should be, the lens through which senior management considers the project. If the provider is a vendor, then the front end of the business lifecycle must account for the differing business views of the owner and the vendor. This can be a source of conflict, so it's important to recognize their existence:

DOI: 10.4324/9781003370031-3

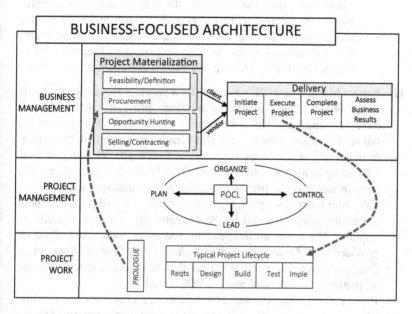

Figure 2.1 Business-focused architecture
Source: First published in Commercial Project Management, 2017

Different Project Perspectives

- Owner View with In-house Provider: Only a feasibility or definition stage is required. The project must meet the owner's need, be defined, and be confirmed as offering a worthwhile return on investment. The project can then immediately be initiated, executed, and completed. After completion, the owner will seek to confirm the business expectations have been met.
- Owner View with Vendor Provider: If a vendor is hired as provider, then the owner requires an additional procurement stage prior to initiation. This usually entails further work on the existing feasibility study to firm up a set of requirements for inclusion in a request for proposal (RFP), the selection of the vendor, and contracting.
- Vendor View: A disciplined view of the business lifecycle is extremely important for the vendor. Project materialization from the vendor's viewpoint is segmented into opportunity hunting, sales, and contracting. The delivery stages represent a common framework but with some variance in client/vendor perspective.

The vendor's business issues boil down to ensuring a progressive project commitment, a full understanding of risk, and a competitive bid that includes fair profit. Project delivery must then be profitable. The delivery stages – initiate, execute, complete, and assess – include the primary elements for vendor and client collaboration.

(2) Project Management. This is naturally a provider responsibility but is ubiquitous. It is therefore important owners, providers, and vendors all have the same view. This domain must *not* be interpreted as a sequential set of management phases. This causes confusion with the natural business and project work lifecycles and invites fruitless debate over competing frameworks such as PMBOK®, PRINCE2®, and others. The domain suggests the parties recognize project management as essentially four functions – plan, organize, control, and lead (POCL). These are easily recognized and invoked repetitively and pragmatically as required. The numerous deliverables, processes, tools, and techniques provided by PM standards such as *A Guide to the Project Management Body of Knowledge (PMBOK®)*,[1] can then be assessed, agreed upon by all parties, and integrated into the POCL model.

(3) Project Work. This is always, by definition, a provider responsibility. The work is usually guided by use of a methodology determined by the provider as suitable for the project. The need for a common understanding of the work is mostly important at the level of the project lifecycle phases, a chief component of methodology. These phases are used as a basis for project go/no, costing forecasts, scheduling, and approvals. There are many different lifecycles, so phases are not universal. It is essential to share and agree on the chosen lifecycle with all participants.

Note the work domain in Figure 2.1 illustrates only one project lifecycle of many in common usage, such as waterfall, iterative, and agile. In the history of IT, these have been referred to as development lifecycles, or application lifecycles. Both are synonymous with the term 'project lifecycle' now mainly used in PM texts.

The business and project lifecycles are different. The dashed arrow in Figure 2.1 shows the execution stage embracing *all* the project lifecycle, apart from a small prologue where project work is needed to supply technical information and analysis to the materialization stage.

A Business Lifecycle

Apart from clearly delineating the three domains of a project, the most important feature of the architecture is the specification of a business lifecycle. This becomes the framework for the construction of the Delivery Organization and its required elements. Lifecycles are a strong conceptual part of project management and can be designed to offer different paths through a project. They are a mechanism for management control.

The Concept

We are familiar with the concept of lifecycles in the project context. Project managers are problem-solvers who use models and frameworks derived from their own and others' experience to solve the big problem of how to deliver the project. One of the oldest tools of project management is the project lifecycle, discussed in detail later in this chapter. Its value is in segmenting a project into technical phases which progressively elaborate the broad requirements of the owner into a product that can be built. It seems reasonable to use the same concept to highlight and manage the business interests that encapsulate the project. The first observation is that business is concerned with a much broader scope than simply executing the work from requirements through to building the product. The project lifecycle is primarily focused on managing the work of the project team. We need to integrate project execution into a broader framework more suited to business considerations. These considerations, neglected for too long, demand the establishment of a financial framework and proper accountabilities, an assessment of owner risk and benefit, the ongoing approval of measurable execution work, a clear demonstration that what has been paid for has indeed been delivered, and finally an assurance that the benefit promised has been gathered. This demands the introduction of an all-encompassing business lifecycle which subsumes the project lifecycle. We must also ensure the project execution lifecycle used by the project team is 'tweaked' to accommodate the needs of the business.

The provider, whether in-house or vendor, inevitably uses the technical project lifecycle to frame their reports and analyses for the owner. Care must be taken to ensure these reports are meaningful. Once the project is launched, the owner wants to know in plain language that the project has been set up for success, the contract is practical, the work is meeting cost and schedule milestones, all obligations are being met, and deliverables are signed off. The owner must also be adequately informed to fulfil their responsibility for immediate and long-term decisions. Throughout, the owner's perspective is dominated by funds committed and level of risk. The owner has the most financial stake in the project and requires accurate reporting on their interests to hold the provider accountable for the agreed financial constraints.

Another rationale for introducing a simple, overarching business lifecycle, as shown in Figure 2.2, is to give the owner tangible control over

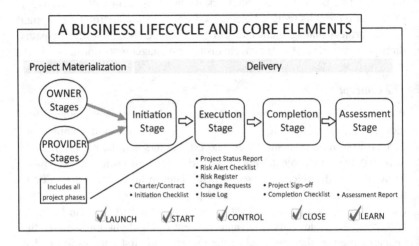

Figure 2.2 A business lifecycle and core elements

the destiny of the project. Oversight of this lifecycle by the owner allows for formal approval of the business case for the project, officially delegating the work to the provider, providing go/no-go decisions at formal status checkpoints, engagement during completion for project sign-off, and the final assessment of business results. The lifecycle is universal, repeatable, and consistent.

The experienced reader might be wondering if the foregoing implies the use of a business lifecycle methodology. No, it doesn't. A methodology includes a comprehensive set of tools such as detailed phase descriptions, process hierarchy and input, process, output (IPO) charts, deployment flowcharts, deliverable templates, and supporting techniques and checklists. The lifecycle in Figure 2.2 identifies four delivery stages, the prime purpose of each stage, and the ten core elements supporting the lifecycle. With the added content of this guide, this is sufficient structure for the average Delivery Organization. Vendor firms, whose business interests totally dominate, may refer to *Commercial Delivery Methodology*[2] if formal methodology is of interest.

Path Overview

The materialization stage is pre-project and rarely viewed as offering opportunity for collaborative processes. The owner and provider are on different paths, operating in parallel.

Project genesis involves early requirements work by the owner and an organization-dependent process to determine priority and budgeting of delivery. If delivery is in-house, the in-house provider provides analytic and technical skills during the prologue stage of the project, but their delivery responsibility only begins at initiation. If the owner seeks a vendor as provider, things become more complicated. Procurement activity must be put in motion, requiring formality and precise protocols. Despite this, the owner is often dragged into interaction with prospective vendors during their own pre-delivery selling and bid preparation work.

Vendor adaptations of the materialization stage provide a tailored framework for managing the bid/no-bid decision, creating and approving the proposal for a deliverable project, and negotiating the contract. These lifecycle stages are operated by the delivery manager.

When a vendor is finally selected, the project still cannot start until a contract is agreed upon and signed. Both owner and provider ensure their interests are being properly represented and agree with obligations being written into the contract.

Collaboration can now be specified as the project enters the common delivery stages of the lifecycle, defined as initiation, execution, and completion. A final assessment stage also has elements that can be reviewed jointly.

The delivery path ensures setting the project up for success during initiation, the provision of risk assessments and business forecasts at formal status checkpoints, completion of project sign-off according to agreed criteria, and final assessment of business results. It is repeatable and consistent, using documents and stage controls commandeered from project management concepts. The core documents are recognizable as project management deliverables (the PM is responsible), but they are specifically designed for the owner with an emphasis on business and contractual issues, control of risk, and funding commitments.

The work of a vendor PM is complicated by the added demands to operate within two organizations (the client and the vendor firm), to make a profit, and to adhere to the terms of the contract. Conflict of interest can come into play, if not in reality, then certainly in perception. And this raises a new complexity of business management; the fact senior vendor management, like the client, has their own different interests in business and contractual issues, risks, and funding commitments.

Note in Figure 2.2 that the execution stage of the delivery path encloses the entire project lifecycle where the technical work of the project is conducted by the PM and team. Thus, this business framework is independent of the type of product, the industry, the number of project phases, or even the project lifecycle itself.

A Universal Project Management Model

Practitioners have learned how to create a shared view of the project by applying the project lifecycle and template specifications for each phase. Can we emulate this and create a shared view of the work of the PMs and those in leadership positions on the project? Without this understanding, miscommunications and conflict can arise. Or sometimes a retreat into the silo to just get on with the job as one understands it.

The problem is not really in the details. The procedures and techniques of project management are well known. The confusion I see arises from the packaging adopted by different standards groups and other third parties. Much of this arises from the temptation to conceptualize project management as a series of processes or phases and the packaging rarely alters this misconception.

Many providers have adopted the packaging from PRINCE2®, PMBOK®, or a proprietary system, or their own in-house project management methodology. Many have spent thousands of dollars investing in it. Is this a material issue? If the provider is in-house, probably not. But for vendors trained in an alternative, it's a challenge.

Presuming reasonableness, the vendor must expect to follow the in-house process. It's probably required by the contract. If the vendor has adopted a universal model and trained under this framework, adapting to the client is not difficult, though of course it would be much easier if the client has also adopted the universal model. That is why it is a component of the Delivery Organization.

The Four-Function Model

When working under the hood, the moving parts of project management are pretty much all the same. Nonetheless, frameworks are important as they condition our interpretation and are hard to shake off when one has been trained to see things a certain way. It's difficult to believe one is driving a Porsche if it looks like a VW Beetle. The question is: what base level of abstraction of project management is truly universal? The answer, I believe, is to represent project management as a set of functions, not a set of processes, and certainly not a lifecycle. This is confirmed by my own and many others' experience and has been influenced by a definition of project management I was impressed with many years ago. It is not in any standard literature I can recall, but here it is, and I commend it:

> *Project management is a structured approach to plan, organize, control, and lead the work of the project to meet project objectives.*

This reflects a productive view of the PM's job as it explains inclusively what the PM does in terms of four functions and exactly why he or she does it. The definition names those functions – plan, organize, control, and lead (POCL) – and they can be universally agreed upon. They are repetitive and never-ending, as implied in Figure 2.3, and never to be confused with a rigid phase-by-phase lifecycle framework.

Project management training becomes more accessible through an explanation of these four functions (though they are intuitively obvious), and then moving to the details of techniques, procedures, and deliverables which support execution of the function. The non-specialist members of the DO only need a description of the model and explanations to back up their intuition.

Another way of thinking about this concept of project management is to envision the PM continuously juggling daily duties between POCL functions. Obviously, the emphasis placed on a specific function depends upon the deliverables being worked on and the current phase of the project. If the project is wrapping up a requirements phase and a project plan is being prepared, then the bulk of the day goes to planning, with the occasional hour or two on organizing. But the next day may bring a working session with the sponsor when it is discovered expectations are misaligned, and departments have conflicting objectives. Now the PM must show leadership. In due course, plans are baselined, and the emphasis moves to controlling, but details must still be worked on, and variances resolved, so a day or two each week still goes to planning.

Simplifying project management as a set of functions is not throwing the baby out with the bathwater. The only real change is the bathtub. All the essential PM processes, deliverables, techniques, and checklists remain, but are now deployed to support commonly agreed functions and promote flexibility, communication, and collaboration between client and vendor PMs.

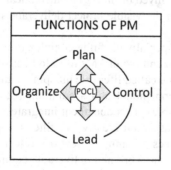

Figure 2.3 Functions of project management

Integrating With the Project Work

The first formal benefit of the POCL view of project management is how natural it is to integrate project management with the project work. If it's thought of as a 'competing' lifecycle, it doesn't seem compatible.

Although PM standards have many benefits and over the past 20 years have resulted in appreciation and respect for the PM role, they have unfortunately contributed to the perception project management exists in its own universe and is disconnected from the work of the project. Most texts on project management barely acknowledge that there is a team of human beings out there whose work actually *is* the project! Their activities are distinguished by the production of deliverables to meet the phase objectives. With the functional view of project management, it's natural to ask: what management function(s) is currently best applied to ensure activities meet objectives? The question after that deals with what tools can help (processes, techniques, etc.).

Thinking "do I need to plan, organize, control or lead?" is the right PM reaction to a project situation, rather than being distracted trying to synchronize incompatible lifecycles, or passively defining PM as a tool, when it should be an active management function. Frameworks are important.

Integrating Project Deliverables

Much of the periodic work of the PM involves preparing a document (aka deliverable). Commonplace examples are laying out the direction and needs of the project to produce the project plan and assessing status and correcting aberrations to create the status report. Thus, the PM supports many functions through documents. To integrate project management into the project work, these documents should be managed in the same way as the team's deliverables, with the added rationale of categorizing the responsible PM function. They are not hived off into some theoretical project management universe, remote from the visible project deliverables. They are a part of the project.

This approach is especially useful in complex project structures where vendor, client, and subcontractor PMs need to be brought into collaboration. Using a technique called lifecycle mapping, a document is prepared using the four-function model and a common list of required project management deliverables. This document integrates the work of all PMs into the lifecycle phases and clearly identifies the person responsible. This technique enforces a common view of project management by all parties and integrates the work and deliverable commitments of all contributing PMs.

Project Lifecycle

The project lifecycle is a useful and widespread technique of project management and one of the oldest. The lifecycle is simply a sequence of defined phases. The work of each phase of the project lifecycle is organized to meet the objectives of the phase and to develop the phase deliverables. The phase generally employs resources of the same type. Each phase has clear completion criteria and provides data for project cost/benefit re-evaluation, so the project receives progressive commitment through the lifecycle.

Project lifecycles have been designed for work in a specific industry or area of application. This might be construction, electronics, pharmaceuticals, software, aviation, and others. An in-house provider is often well-versed in such a lifecycle, and the owner will probably have sufficient familiarity to permit good communications. Should a vendor provider be contracted, it is likely the technical practitioners of the vendor provide their own methods. If so, potential incompatibilities with the in-house team must be resolved. All participants must enjoy a common understanding of how the project is sequenced because that is the platform for management of the project and communications of status. It is a foundation for project management collaboration.

Classic Example

In the early days when project management methodology was developing, the lifecycle was almost always depicted as a sequential, step-by-step series of phases following a progression of increasing detail from initial requirements through design, build, and implement. This is still common and is chosen here as a base for study by readers who are unfamiliar with project work.

Such lifecycles are colloquially referred to as *waterfall* lifecycles, meaning one phase must be completed before the next is started. This emphasizes thoroughness and quality during each phase. In a waterfall, a return to a previous phase would suggest a mistake had been made and must be rectified. Figure 2.4 shows an example of a waterfall or classic lifecycle.

The type of diagram chosen to illustrate this schedule is called a Gantt chart, and the idea of a waterfall is taken from the 'flow' of deliverables from one phase to the next. This diagram can also show milestones graphically as a black diamond. In the example, a go/no-go milestone is clearly shown at the end of the General Design phase. If the lifecycle is used consistently across all parts of the project, and participants in the project understand how to interpret a Gantt chart, this becomes a great tool to promote communication and project integration.

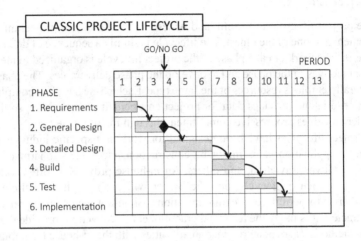

Figure 2.4 Classic project lifecycle

Source: First published in Commercial Project Management, 2017

Lifecycle Variations

Sometimes, to reduce the project duration, waterfall phases may be over-lapped, though this naturally increases risk. The phase completion criteria are consciously relaxed, and the next phase started early. This version of the waterfall is called *fast tracking*.

Another type of project lifecycle encountered in certain application areas is the *iterative* lifecycle. The iterative lifecycle partitions the product into components, so the design phase is kept open as successive components are worked on. When a component is designed, it moves right away into the build phase, without waiting for design work to complete on the remaining components. Thus, there are as many iterations as there are product compo-nents. There is added risk in this approach because component interactions can lead to rework on components thought to be finished.

Project lifecycle designers have taken the concepts of the iterative life-cycle and further refined it into a spiral lifecycle and more recently into the agile lifecycle. Consultants, product developers, and others with expertise in the application area have taken the concept of the project lifecycle, be it waterfall, iterative, spiral, or agile and generated full-blown methodologies offered for sale in the marketplace.

This proliferation of project approaches has tended to blur phase bounda-ries and objectives, and weakened the discipline required to successfully use any lifecycle. I believe it must be restored to a place of prominence in joint owner/provider planning because, combined with the project management model, it is a key to successful project integration.

Silo Mentality

The silo model is a well-known metaphor for the constraints of functional organizations. These constraints may be encouraged by the organization or may be self-imposed for numerous reasons. As Figure 2.5 illustrates, in a silo world the requests for decisions or initiatives involving two or more silos must be approved by the common authority.

Resources within the silo report in a hierarchical structure to a functional manager. Work requests involving staff in another silo must ascend to the point of common authority before being passed down again to the intended staff. For example, employee A in the diagram has a work request for employee B. For this to occur, A must escalate the request through A's hierarchy to the first point of common authority with employee B. This is senior manager C, who must then transmit the request down the hierarchy to employee B whereupon some negotiation will occur while A waits.

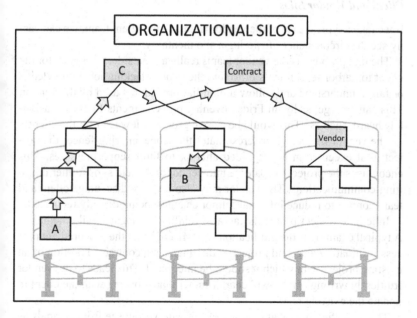

Figure 2.5 Organizational silos

Barriers to Project Integration

Other characteristics can also indicate a silo mentality. Objectives may be framed in narrow terms so silo workers lose sight of the common goal of the larger organization. Team identification may be fostered to such a degree that those outside the silo are seen as outsiders. Working conditions or management policies may result in excessive internal competition, or a culture of blame or scapegoating, or uneven accountabilities that erode trust and collaboration outside the unit.

Of course, the matrix structure in Figure 1.1 is used by project management as one attempts to engage functional resources to meet an objective outside their own group. Other solutions include establishing task forces and liaison committees, using temporary secondments, setting up self-empowered teams, and even abandoning a hierarchical functional organization altogether.

Resource A and resource B silos are examples within the same organization, but often a third silo effect can occur with an external party. Frequent and quite serious situations can arise between the client and the contracted vendor, and the only common authority is the contract.

Client and Vendor Silos

If we take a typical case of the vendor team and the client team, we can easily see the circumstances fostering a silo mentality.

The first problem is the vendor teams really are outsiders. It's easy for the client to harbor resentments or to find the vendor lacking local knowledge or fail to understand and follow unfamiliar procedures used by the vendor. This can emerge, sadly, in Friday evening pub comments I have occasionally heard, such as "This would be a great project if it wasn't for the client!"

The vendor frequently underestimates the scope and ring-fences the project as it executes in a misguided attempt to limit scope pressures. This encourages the project to coalesce into vendor and client silos further inhibiting communications. The vendor may also actively discourage client and team contact to reduce informal 'minor changes' being directly requested.

Inflexible project protocols can also reinforce a negative silo mentality. A typical example is the implication by PMBOK® that the procurement process is initiating a second project, rather than a subcontracted portion of an existing project with which it should be integrated. This leads to the vendor fruitlessly writing 'their own' charter rather than working with the client to update the existing one.

The silo effect is probably a fact of life, but we can see from an analysis of these problems more must be done to supplement the matrix structure. The effect can't be eliminated, but it can be improved.

Owner/Provider Balance

There is a natural dichotomy between the owner and provider which gives any project a sense of tension. But if we redraw this to emphasize the need for balance, then it aligns nicely with a fundamental principle of quality management governing any transaction between two parties. There is always a supplier and an acceptor, whose acceptance is an important quality process. In a civilized economy, there are transaction rules to follow, and responsibilities to which both parties should adhere. The common transaction we are concerned with in project management is the provision and acceptance of a deliverable, which may be a document, a service, or a system. It is important to adhere to the principle of balance between the responsibilities of owner and provider.

This model lays down a concept to which both provider and owner can subscribe. I believe this is universal and, in Figure 2.6, I have listed the responsibilities generally applicable. Though they may occasionally be modified, the intent is to achieve owner/provider balance.

The first responsibility of the owner is to draft and agree with the provider on the criteria under which the deliverable will be accepted. This critical step is often done well in advance of the delivery date. With this information, the provider can initiate work, provide a delivery schedule, and communicate the status of the work periodically.

At the point of handover to the owner, the provider must account for any remaining deficiencies and the intended action. The owner must then assess these deficiencies, including others found during inspection or testing, and

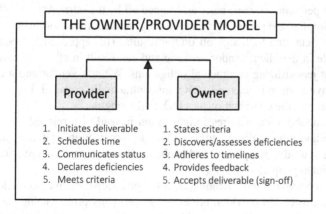

Figure 2.6 The owner/provider model

Source: First published in Commercial Project Management, 2017

provide feedback. Timelines established for this activity must be kept, or the overall delivery schedule will slip.

Finally, the provider must act on the deficiencies or negotiate exceptions so the criteria are met, and the owner must sign an acceptance.

This model has contractual significance when using a vendor as provider of services. In most services, at least those for which fixed-price deliverables have been contracted, the client will insist on fixed schedule dates and quality (or residual defect) standards. Many risks attach to the vendor in agreeing to these requirements, and considerable time can be spent in negotiating. Whereas the terms holding a vendor to contractual commitments are meticulous, there is much less scrutiny given to the client's obligations. This can be rectified using the owner/provider balance as a basis for drafting reasonable terms and conditions for deliverable acceptance.

Creating the Delivery Organization

These models can lead us to solutions, many of which are intended to enable or mandate collaboration at the core of the DO. In most cases, these are changes to a style of working, giving attention to techniques previously ignored, and in some cases provision of pre-designed procedures to be prescribed when projects are initiated. The cost to achieve this is minimal.

The idea of collaboration to achieve better results is hardly original. Exhortations to collaborate have been heard before. Unfortunately, often missing are tangible and specific techniques to help participants, many of whom are unknown to each other. In their absence, collaboration starts to receive only lip service and eventually falls by the roadside.

Collaboration must be active and participatory. It does not simply mean work is performed by one party and signed off by the other. Active collaboration implies the parties agree to a jointly defined allocation of work and management, and both sign off on the results. This approach is especially valuable in the client/vendor scenario and can result in efficiency savings without jeopardizing contractual obligations. When a vendor and a client who have both implemented a DO are contractually engaged, I optimistically refer to the combination as a DO, in the singular!

So, collaboration requires formalization instead of a relaxed 'let's just meet in a group and discuss things' kind of process. Without it, any success will be sporadic, temporary, and probably based on rare combinations of exceptional people.

Collaboration is only meaningful if the prerequisites have been adopted by both owner and provider, preferably *prior* to any project being contemplated. (That is the crux of this guide.) Thus, when a project is contemplated, communication is immediate and repetitive groundwork is unnecessary. All that is required is immediate activation, or in some cases a 'fill out the blanks' approach so all parties can take joint responsibility for efficient project delivery.

Here is the summary of the foundations for collaboration concluded from the preceding discussion. This is expanded and formalized into either techniques, reviews, processes, or documents in the next chapter.

Foundations for Collaboration

(1) A Business-Focused Lifecycle: Drives incremental commitment, risk management, and project business and contract management. The joint lifecycle discourages the silo mentality, makes sense to both owner and provider, and avoids those activities truly internal or confidential.

(2) A Universal Project Management Framework: Provides all parties with a functional view of project management based on a common understanding of project planning, organization, control, and leadership. This drives project integration, management communication, and PM action.

(3) A Common Project Lifecycle: Supports execution and drives project integration, owner/provider communication, and collaborative deliverable assignments.

In addition, note these collaborative frameworks rely on owner support for sponsorship and provider support for project team building, both discussed in a later chapter. These don't necessarily demand collaboration, but they do enable the Delivery Organization.

Notes

1 PMI®. 2013. *A Guide to the Project Management Body of Knowledge (PMBOK® Guide)*, Fifth Edition, Project Management Institute.
2 Hornby, Robin. 2019. *Commercial Delivery Methodology*, Google Books ebook.

3 Stages of the Business Lifecycle

The stages fall naturally into two segments. The first, project materialization, is rarely viewed as a collaborative stage and is variable depending upon usage of an in-house or vendor provider. The second stage, project delivery, is the focus of the guide and specifies collaborative elements which improve the owner's business control and the provider's efficiency.

Elements for Collaboration

- Reviews or Walkthroughs: Used to gain a common understanding or to decide/approve.
- Mandatory Processes: Drive active collaboration.
- Techniques: Also drive active collaboration in the production of deliverables, definition of accountabilities, etc.
- Documents: Report project status in meaningful terms, record collaborative decisions, the results of joint processes or techniques, or any management report issued by consensus.

The business lifecycle is the framework for housing these elements and although some of them find a dual purpose in the technical project lifecycle which guides the project team, the business lifecycle is very different. Its stages of initiate, execute, complete, and assess are naturally understood by the owner, who can easily follow the standard template given for each stage: Objective, overall purpose, start and exit criteria, description, and the usage of each DO element within the stage.

The introduction of the business lifecycle and the collaborative use of the elements described in this chapter represent a paradigm shift in the perceived role of the PM. Traditionally, the PM has been obliged to act as an authoritarian in order to create an environment that recognizes the legitimacy and importance of various project disciplines. Many PMs are unwilling to adopt

DOI: 10.4324/9781003370031-4

this role, preferring to maintain a comfortable relationship with the owner, who has not perceived the importance or the self-interest, of engaging in project administration or execution issues. These may have previously been ignored, or seen only as a concern of the PM. The collaborative approach to these matters changes the role of the PM from unwelcome instigator of new rules and procedures to skilled and knowledgeable partner of the owner in a joint enterprise to create something new and of benefit to the company.

Project Materialization Stage

The objective is to launch a feasible, deliverable project. The stages are identified in the architecture. Collaboration is not significant as a procedural criterion in these early stages.

Formal propositions, or simply suggestions for projects, are usually offered to the authorizing body for departmental capital expenditures, or simply to an owner who might perceive a benefit.

The vehicle for assessing the proposition and outlining a potential project is a brief feasibility or preliminary requirements study, including a high-level cost/benefit analysis. This is undertaken by business and technical analysts supplied by the owner's organization, or more likely seconded by the provider. At this point, there is no formal project or any PM, though the provider may assign the delivery manager to maintain a watching brief and provide continuity. This is a prologue to the eventual project, should it come to life.

The company then goes through a series of idiosyncratic processes to determine if (1) the promised benefit justifies continuance, (2) the time-scale of the project can meet the need for the delivery of benefits, and (3) funding will be available. These critical business deliberations can entail a quasi-collaborative arena, such as a planning committee involving owners and providers, where numerous criteria are applied to competing projects to determine priorities. The results are laid out in a strategic plan (updated annually). The project is then quiescent until initiation, unless the project is to be contracted, in which case the procurement process precedes it.

Owner/Provider Guidance

(1) Customer Services Manager. Some large companies formalize the owner/provider link by introducing a liaison position with each departmental owner. A key responsibility is to actively canvas the owner for opportunities to apply technology. This aspect of the role mirrors the vendor sales executive during opportunity hunting.

Client/Vendor Guidance

(1) Vendor Pre-Sales. The early stages of materialization operated by the vendor are opportunity hunting and selling. The vendor's sales executives are trained to follow up on their firm's marketing initiatives and promotions to engage with would-be owners or sponsors. Should this resolve into a solid project opportunity then the degree of collaboration depends upon whether the client seeks competitive proposals. In most cases, the client decides competition is required and the nature of the competitive environment then precludes significant information sharing between the client and, most likely, *multiple* vendors. The process can be very lengthy and takes unpredictable turns, though usually results in the publishing of an RFP.

(2) Procurement. A client's decision to engage a vendor as provider involves a procurement process. Typically, an RFP is assembled and circulated to interested vendors. A formal selection process is followed to determine a winning vendor who is then engaged in contract negotiations.

(3) Contract as the Bridge to Delivery. The contracting of a vendor as provider is a bridge into delivery. It replaces the development of a project charter during initiation for the in-house case. To reflect reality, the preliminary discussions on contracting during proposal evaluation are considered project materialization. The selection of a bid winner starts the initiation stage, and so the serious negotiation of a contract agreement falls into initiation. Procurement, pre-sales, and contracting are more fully explored in the final chapter, *The Future of Collaboration*.

(4) The Statement of Work Commitment. The vendor's proposal includes a technical section usually called a Statement of Work (SOW). If accepted, the SOW becomes a technical appendix to the contract (called a 'Schedule') and provides a foundation for all the commitments and obligations being made by the vendor. It is an interpretation of the feasibility or requirements study included in the RFP, almost certainly updated by additional prologue effort from the vendor's bid team. Although seen as a technical project document, and often stripped of financial data at the client's request, it has business significance as the basis for the project estimates. Different names are used for this key contract document:

- Statement of Work (SOW)
- Scope of Work (SOW)
- Technical Specifications
- Project Requirements

- Project Definition
- Preliminary Project Plan

To many, it is simply seen as 'the contract' because it represents the scope of the project, the commitment for delivery, and the baseline for all that follows.

Project Delivery Stages

It is in the delivery stages where collaboration can be given serious attention. It begins with an agreement on frameworks, in particular, the business lifecycle. If the parties enjoy a shared understanding and agree on a collaborative framework, then the bulk of the setup time can be spent reviewing the elements for each of the collaborative stages, filling out the blanks, making joint decisions, participating in walkthroughs, and preparing agreed joint documents.

This section describes a usage template for the elements in each stage. They are discussed from a generic owner/provider perspective. Specific hints are included under the heading *Owner/Provider Guidance*, and issues specific to the client/vendor case are discussed under *Client/Vendor Guidance*. As sequenced, elements are given the designation DOn where n is from 1 to 22. This is indicative of the order in which they are encountered, but the sequence of development is not prescribed.

These elements are the cornerstone of the collaborative approach. Most may be considered administrative; the reminder drawn from three professional practices is expanded in the following chapter where the relevant elements are explained in more detail.

Initiation Stage

The objective is to start the project with barriers to success removed. The essence of initiation is speed and finding clarity. During these early days of potential chaos, enough direction, structure, and order must be established to allow real work by the project team to start efficiently.

The initiation stage starts with the appointment of a PM, and the first job is to prepare the project charter in collaboration with the sponsor. Like all collaborative documents, it requires a template provided by the DO.

Exit from the initiation stage specifically requires the signing of the project charter (or contract) and completion of all items on the initiation checklist.

Initiation Elements

The following techniques, reviews, processes, and documents are specified for the DO:

DO1 The Project Charter. The template specifies, at a minimum, why the project is needed, the benefits expected, and the nature of the problems to be solved or opportunities to be exploited. Business and project objectives are laid out, basic requirements are listed, alternative ways of proceeding are discussed, and a recommended approach with expected costs and schedule are presented. Specific resources are identified, and the management roles and responsibilities are defined. More comprehensive content could include risk, scope description, deliverable list, constraints, and assumptions. The data collected during project materialization form significant input and depending on how recent they are and how complete, the charter may be quickly assembled. This document is the mandate for the project and the PM. It is authorized by the sponsor.

DO2 Joint Management Agreements (Owner/Provider). From my experience, the project executes better when owner and provider(s) sit down during initiation and agree with the basic standards and protocols relevant to the project. For the practicing DO, this need not be complicated and is an early collaborative process. The template agenda includes the joint project processes to be used; the key techniques to be used; joint practices to be used; and any procedure development required. In short, the tools of the DO to be used during execution are reviewed, modified, and agreed upon.

DO3 Project Lifecycle Walkthrough. The architecture model identifies the third domain as the work of the project team and is governed by the chosen development methodology. Good collaboration requires an understanding by all parties of the chosen project lifecycle. There are many structures for project phases (waterfall, iterative, agile, etc.), and the decision is technical and usually made by the provider. But steps are needed to ensure all parties do understand the project's structure. At a walkthrough, the provider leads the owner through a description of the project phases. Emphasis is on business-related topics such as the purpose, the key phase documents, the support provided for go/no-go decisions, and important approvals.

DO4 Project Lifecycle Mapping. This is probably the most important collaboration tool for owner and provider managers during initiation as it enforces understanding and adherence to both the project lifecycle and the POCL model of project management and encompasses the entire list of project documents. This tool, in one table, ties together the responsibilities of the owner and provider(s) for development of PM documents by project phase and by project management function (POCL). Originally a tool to assist the technical team plan their deliverables, it has been extended to project management and business-focused documents to further encourage project integration. An example is shown in Table 6.3.

DO5 Project Risk Register. One of the recommended tools of collaboration is a joint approach to risk management. Initiation is a good place to begin the development of a risk register and possible mitigations based on a risk event model. The register is developed over several sessions. The most usual technique is to first use a brainstorming approach to identify project risks. Next, each risk is assigned a severity and probability. Finally, those risks with the highest impact on the project are assigned mitigation. The first version may be limited to collaboration between more senior owner/provider personnel, but updates during later stages include members from the expanded team.

DO6 Risk Factor Checklist. Based on an innovative risk planning model, project risk is seen as present in the environment and uses the metaphor of *risk factors* as daggers continually attacking the links binding the project to its objectives. These are not unforeseen 'bolts from the blue' as speculated in the event model but can be predefined by analysis. The two methods are complementary. Risk factors are deemed to lurk in the universal *facets* of the project class, based on the nature of the application and implementation environment. These are used to build a standard checklist of factors for each class of application and an example is shown in Table 6.1.

DO7 Responsibility Assignment Matrix (RAM). During initiation, the parties also share information regarding the responsibilities and delegated authorities of the project principles. Project friction is reduced if people have a mutual understanding of their responsibilities, and those in equivalent positions have been delegated similar or matching authorities. This counteracts the tendency to work in silos and helps maintain business consistency between owner and provider. A useful tool for this is the responsibility assignment matrix. This is a detailed tool which makes a type of responsibility assignment using a PARIS code as demonstrated in Table 6.4. The matrix places individuals on the top horizontal axis and deliverable (or activity) down the left vertical axis. The PARIS code is at the intersection.

DO8 The Initiation Checklist. The PM will also be busy during initiation completing several tasks and taking decisions to get the project off to a clean start. A checklist helps to ensure all elements are dealt with.

The checklist template includes the items of importance to the owner and the provider and is to be completed to the satisfaction of both parties as confirmed during the review. Relevant items include the aforementioned initiation elements, plus status reporting, short-term milestones, resources, acceptance criteria, stakeholders, team briefing, and kickoff meeting.

Owner/Provider Guidance

(1) Related Integration Techniques. Promoting project integration and making sure both provider and owner have the same view of the project is a real concern during initiation. The DO7 RAM and the technique of DO4 Lifecycle Mapping are good for this. Other techniques include the careful, explicit statement of objectives and sharing between all parties, clarity of role between PM(s) and sponsor, shared success definitions, sponsored opportunities for social interaction, and a good communications plan.

(2) Project Plan. The experienced reader may be wondering why I have not included the project plan in my list of collaborative initiation documents. There are two reasons:

- It is better to maintain clear PM responsibility. Although there are clear points of consultation and input from the owner, and secondary content may be collaborative, the project plan is unequivocally the PM's document. It is submitted by the PM to the sponsor, to operations, to functional heads, and to others for approval.
- The plan may not be completed during initiation. Serious project planning takes time. For a large project, it could be several months. Planning requires supplementing the work done by the team during the prologue with a more thorough requirements phase, or whatever is specified as the first phase of the chosen project lifecycle. So, with the PM working serious hours on developing a project plan, and the project team working weeks or months on requirements, it is ridiculous to say the project has not started.

(3) Optionality. DO2 Agreements and DO3 Walkthroughs may not always be required for the in-house provider case because the parties are a single Delivery Organization, and a review may not be necessary.

Client/Vendor Guidance

(1) Project Manager Appointment. The selection of the vendor is the effective trigger for initiation, and a PM should immediately be appointed

by the vendor and ratified by the client. The client will also complete any activities and documents required by their procurement process when a contract is awarded.

(2) Contract. The first job is to review the contract, ensure it is understood, and is signed by both parties. Contracts for fixed-price controlled work will usually include a preliminary version of a full project plan as a schedule (appendix). It is not possible to claim the contract as a collaborative document, unlike the DO1 Project Charter which it replaces. The adversarial system governs contract law, and this generally becomes the underlying tone of contract development. Issues can arise from selection of the incorrect contract type, inefficient terms and conditions, and excessive start-up delay. Many terms can impede subsequent collaborative working and should be scrutinized.

The shift from the sales focus to delivery and an increasingly collaborative operational mode occurs when the contract is signed, and the PMs are appointed. However, if contract agreement cannot be reached then contract negotiation terminates, and the process restarts with the runner-up.

(3) Extension to Joint Agreements. During DO2 Agreements, the purpose of the review is to sort out procedural and working issues at the *beginning* of the project, rather than when things go wrong. This process is extra valuable in the client/vendor case, and the recommended agenda could be expanded to include agreement on the status of the baseline, criteria for phase completion, matching of vendor/client PM delegations, and clarity on what constitutes inappropriate communication occurring outside of the communications plan.

(4) Extension to Initiation Checklist. The business perspective of the vendor will require an adaptation or confidential addendum to DO8 Checklist to address items such as cost budget, margin, contingency, cash flow plan, time reporting, revenue recognition plan, reserve allocation, etc. These are essential to the vendor business workings of the project. Such adaptations are necessarily outside the collaborative theme.

(5) Culture. The project integration elements which dominate initiation are key to creating a blended client/vendor team who will work well together. Nonetheless, it is likely these organizations have developed different organizational cultures, so during initiation it is beneficial for the respective PMs to meet informally and discuss the topic.

Execution Stage

The objective is to ensure business control of the project, which now begins in earnest. The execution stage encapsulates all phases of the project lifecycle agreed upon by charter or contract.

Execution is where the real work of the project is performed and the interests of all stakeholders, particularly the owner, are centered on ensuring the project unfolds as planned. Impetus for collaboration is derived from plans and commitments made by the parties during initiation, so collaboration agreements continue into execution.

Execution reports must usefully and accurately reflect business conditions and allow business decisions to be made rationally, using logical templates. In the normal multi-project environment, the provider's delivery manager takes responsibility to supervise PMs, holds them accountable for their plans, and reviews the project with the owner when appropriate.

Business management during execution includes responding to issues in the monthly project status report, analyzing go/no-go issues in the phase end report, assessing project performance, risk, resource status and utilization, and dealing with budget increases.

Exit from the execution stage is decided primarily by the judgment of the provider who must assess whether all activities to meet delivery commitments have been finished or are in the final stages of completion. Perhaps I can paraphrase the criterion as "the end is in sight". This means all deliverables are believed to be complete or rectification action has been defined.

Execution Elements

The following techniques, reviews, processes, and documents are specified for the DO:

DO9 Project Status Report (for Owner). This is a core document of the execution stage and if there is more than one provider it is produced collaboratively as agreed during lifecycle mapping. It is targeted to the owner and primary stakeholders and is usually issued at month end. The owner does *not* want to see a status report from the vendor *and* from the in-house PM! Important business information includes an overall assessment of performance items like milestones, schedules, red issues, specific cost information such as actual expenditure, value of completed deliverables, budget remaining, estimate to complete, and an overall percent of completion calculated using an agreed formula. This report is reviewed by the provider with the owner at a meeting of the steering committee.

DO10 Risk Alert Checklist. Based on an innovative risk execution model, project risk is forecast based on the present state of leading risk indicators. This common-sense approach to risk management during execution uses a checklist built up by the provider which identifies telltales of looming project trouble in key performance areas. I have standardized the basic areas of performance interest as delivery, financial, owner, and team. For example, a team trouble alert is an increasing level of unplanned overtime. Table 6.2 provides a more detailed example of typical risk alerts. Although originally designed for internal vendor review, this approach is broadened into a collaborative exercise and can be customized for specific owner objectives by adding factors to the checklist, perhaps drawn from the selection in Table 4.3. This process operates as a recurring monthly event facilitated by the PMs.

DO11 Change Management. Change management is recognized as an essential project procedure, designed to maintain control of development while allowing for necessary changes in requirements to be entered into the design. Change requests are mandated as a core input document, usually only raised by stakeholders in a management position, for the attention of the provider who develops an estimate and impact assessment. The provider's administration maintains a log and can issue ongoing reports for the owner. The request is reviewed by a committee of owner and provider personnel specifically to review changes, and is approved, declined, or placed on hold with a defined release provision.

DO12 Issue Management. This is another procedure generally recognized as essential. Good issue management is key to avoid dysfunctional projects. An issue is generally defined as an impediment to project progress or success. Issues can be raised by any manager in the provider or owner team and are forwarded to the PM. It is the PM's responsibility to keep track of issues, determine the root cause, and assign them for resolution. A project document called an issue log tracks all project issues.

DO13 Decision Requests. Decision requests are not essential but as a part of a strong collaborative environment can work very well and contribute to efficient execution. In a poor environment, they can be used either in frustration or as a means of ensuring a record is created of the putative assignment of responsibility. They are not an alternative to a good working relationship between the PM and the sponsor but a means of clarification and communication between all project principals. Because of potential for misuse and creation of negativity, they must be coordinated by the PM and discussed with the requestee before being placed on the file. A decision, incidentally, may also be requested of the PM or other team managers.

DO14 Deliverable Acceptance. A good, pragmatic delivery acceptance procedure is a key component of a well-organized project. A functioning DO recognizes deliverables are really a responsibility of both the provider and the owner. This duality is explained in the section

Owner/Provider Balance, which should be reflected in the procedure. A sign-off formalizes the agreement to accept the deliverable, subject to any caveats or conditions.

DO15 Phase End Report. This is a special version of a status report which includes narrative from the provider dealing with a broader assessment of project performance, stability of the project, risk management status, quality assessment, resourcing issues, severity of unsolved problems, a forecast of whether the project will meet objectives or not, and other items as requested. This report is reviewed by the provider with the owner at a meeting of the steering committee, with a decision logged to continue the work. If this decision cannot be reached, owner and provider will pursue actions as directed by the committee to determine project cancelation or another alternative.

DO16 Delivery Dashboard Report. This summary report is issued for multiple projects by the provider (delivery manager) for business assessment by senior management. The tabular report lists data for each qualifying project and may include identifying information, value, end date, POC% (Percent of Completion), change in POC% during the period, contingency used, risk alerts, and risk trends.

Owner/Provider Guidance

(1) Keep Elements Up to Date. Some initiation documents should be periodically reviewed to ensure they are not out of date. The following are likely to be variable:

- DO5 Risk Register documents risks specific to the project and can be static through a project phase. However, it should be placed on an update cycle, perhaps every 3 months, to reassess risk, probability, severity, overall rank, and mitigation. DO5 Risk Register should not be confused with the DO10 Risk Alert which is a standard set of alerts reviewed monthly during execution, or the DO6 Risk Factor Checklist which is an initial planning tool and is never updated.

- DO7 RAM which establishes responsibilities for each of the project's deliverables is not particularly volatile but should be reviewed and updated as needed. Reasons may include the definition of a new deliverable, or errors to be corrected in the original assignments.

Client/Vendor Guidance

(1) Changes versus Deficiencies. For the vendor, discipline around change request (DO11) submissions is essential to determine whether these

items are defects to be repaired at the vendor's cost or genuine changes to be charged to the client. In a client/vendor environment, it is usual to use another process and a form called a deficiency report to specifically manage items related to suspected product defects.

(2) Risk. The vendor's business and risk management issues differ from the owner's and are also dependent upon type of contract. In addition to joint management of the DO10 Risk Alert, the vendor probably conducts their own independent risk and business reviews.

(3) Financial Specifics. Several of these elements are of more significance in a client/vendor environment than in-house because of financial implications. DO14 Deliverable Acceptance will likely imply a progress payment to the vendor. And DO15 Phase End Report may also have broader political and financial implications, particularly if the findings are trending to negative and cancelation is a possibility. Cancelation charges and performance penalties defined in the contract then must be interpreted. Finally, the DO16 Dashboard Report certainly includes data vital to a vendor's business, such as planned and forecast project margin.

Completion Stage

The objective is to close out the project with attention to all details. Although the work of the project is fundamentally over, moving the project to a state of completion agreed upon between the owner and the provider is rarely a simple and effortless process.

Moving a larger complex project through the completion stage to a successful conclusion can be a major challenge for most PMs. This can differentiate the skilled and experienced PM from an inexperienced colleague. The reasons for this are not hard to imagine. Completion requires the owner to declare satisfaction with the results and to put this sentiment in writing. It's a rare project that executes every requirement precisely and unambiguously, and clearly demonstrates this fact to the owner. And even when that goal is achieved, it is quite usual to discover small shifts in requirements leading to last-minute change requests and other unplanned activities to be worked.

The best marker for transition from execution to completion is an agreement between the provider PM and the owner, identifying activities to move the project from its current status to full completion. This may be thought of as a 'mini' project plan and provides the basis for a controlled method to achieve project sign-off. This should guard against never-ending scope arguments and poorly defined work characterizing the end of large projects, sometimes referred to as the tail of the dragon.

Normal status reporting will continue during this stage, which for large complex projects may require several months as Figure 3.1 implies.

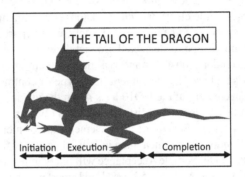

Figure 3.1 The tail of the dragon

Source: First published in Commercial Project Management, 2017

Business management will have a particular interest in completion activities as some work may be beyond the approved estimates. Pressure from approaching deadlines is also increasing, and questions or doubts about the quality of the system may start to be voiced.

Exit from the completion stage is clear and unambiguous – the project is signed off.

Completion Elements

The following techniques, reviews, processes, and documents are specified for the DO:

DO17 Project Sign-off. If a completion mini-plan has been prepared and executed, sign-off becomes simpler, depending only on the completion of all the defined activities. The document is straightforward, usually proffered by the PM who declares the work complete, subject to any agreed exceptions, and then signed by the owner.

DO18 Transition Plan (to Production/Maintenance). After completion of the project, transition into production can commence. This can be a complicated process, depending on the nature of the project, in which case a transition plan is essential. Activities to be identified, estimated, and assigned might include production of a handover report from the project team, provision of special installation tools and assistance, knowledge transfer and tailored training, establishment of organizational and responsibility changes, and definition of new procedures. Commissioning and production planning by the new system owner is also occurring during this stage, as defined by the project lifecycle. One of the questions to be settled during commissioning is the adequacy of arrangements for system maintenance. This includes identification of resources, their training, system documentation, and efficient protocols for the raising, planning, execution, testing, and implementation of maintenance requests.

DO19 Completion Checklist. At the end of every project, there is a formal review to ensure no loose ends are overlooked. The checklist provides guidance on the topics to be covered including official recording of performance against the triple constraint (budget, schedule, scope), quality standards adherence, risk register accounting and closeout, release of team, completion of sign-offs, management control of transition, and archive of project records.

Client/Vendor Guidance

(1) Contract Obligations. It is critical the vendor works with the client to scrutinize contract requirements and acceptance criteria versus actual accomplishments, and then negotiates the path to successful completion and sign-off. This might include adjustments to work or contract.

(2) Production Use. It is also reasonable to incent client engagement by ensuring the contract stipulates no production use of the product is allowed until sign-off. It should also make clear it is an obligation of the client to sign-off, unless review and testing reveal a material defect to be identified in writing within an acceptable period.

(3) Vendor Internal Completions. For a vendor, completion occurs in two stages. The first stage is the signing of the project sign-off by both the vendor and the client. This releases the vendor's obligation (warranty issues excepted) and can trigger the release of staff, subcontractors, and final invoicing. The second stage of completion is internal to the vendor and is represented by the finalization of all project financials, closure of the project accounts, and team assignment reports. This can occur sometime after stage one and is likely monitored by the vendor delivery manager rather than the PM who has by this time been released from the project.

(4) Team Disengagement. In a contracted project, the owner (client) naturally wants to keep the team of experts around as long as possible to work on every potential issue. At the same time, the project team is inclined to defer difficult issues to the last minute. So, you can see why the completion stage can be a drawn-out misery. The '99% complete' syndrome is the most common project disease (see Figure 3.1). It behooves the vendor to be sensitive to client support needs during this period but to protect vendor financial interests by explaining warranty, maintenance, and sustaining engineering provisions. If not explicitly part of the original contract, this work should be funded by a change request or a new contract.

(5) Vendor Completion Checklist. This will doubtless include additional business items such as achievement of actual costs, revenue, and margin versus estimate, broken down by allocation to plan, CRs, and contingency. Opportunities for further business will also be checked out.

Assessment Stage

The objective is to learn, personally and institutionally, from the project experience. So, although the project is signed off and the PM is released from duties, the business lifecycle keeps it alive for one more stage – assessment. In the absence of the PM, this stage is administered by the delivery manager usually 3 or so months after implementation. The owner and provider plan this together.

A major part of this effort is to assess the achievement of the original objectives. These are examined as objectively as possible, using data collected from the project during development and in operation. Both classes of objective are examined – project and business objectives.

The methods used during the project are also evaluated. Were the project phases correctly chosen? Was there a better approach? Were the deliverables of acceptable quality? Was the transition from project team to production usage and support team well conducted? Are there any lessons to be learned for the Delivery Organization?

This stage is complete upon the preparation and acceptance of recommendations for both the owner and the provider. The first set of recommendations covers the system itself, listing any modifications or supplementary procedures to improve the developed system. The second set covers the global environment for development, or the Delivery Organization elements, requiring changes or enhancements to secure more success in the future.

Assessment Elements

The following techniques, reviews, processes, and documents are specified for the DO:

DO20 Satisfaction Survey. The survey technique is an excellent way of garnering feedback from all stakeholders. A questionnaire approach is more cost-efficient, though one-on-one interviews are probably more reliable. The questionnaire asks for opinions on the effectiveness of the project team, the management of owner/provider relationships, the quality of the product, and the reliability of the owner/provider commitments.

DO21 Performance Evaluation. Strengthening future project performance and the abilities of the Delivery Organization require an assessment of the individuals who held material responsibilities for the success of the project. The methods for achieving this are numerous, but the topic is controversial. The section *Performance Management* explores this in more detail. Depending on the culture of the engaged organizations, it might not be feasible to consider staff evaluations as a joint undertaking. However, to solidly define areas where individuals can improve their skills, both viewpoints are useful. Managers involved in the review consider quality of work, relationship ability, communication skills, role specifics (planning, problem-solving, initiative, judgment, etc.), and attention to administration.

DO22 Assessment Report. To maintain the accuracy and discipline of post-project assessments, a standard format for this report is developed. The template might include the following:

Assessment Report Table of Content

- Presentation of Project Data. This includes costs, duration, and effort – in terms of original plan versus actuals achieved.
- Achievement of Objectives. Each of the objectives (usually found in the project charter) is assessed on how well it was achieved, using objective data as much as possible.
- Project Execution Review. A look back over the specific aspects of the project to determine how well they worked. This might include the defined phases, the usefulness and quality of deliverables, how well issues were handled, and strengths or deficiencies of the chosen approach. This would also be the place to record a more detailed assessment of the applicability of the Delivery Organization elements described in this guide.
- Project Operations Review. Putting a system into operation is not always straightforward and can sometimes blemish the success of an otherwise well-done project. Data for this part of the assessment can be gained from special workshops, interviews, or questionnaires. The aim is to determine how smoothly the system went into production and whether, in retrospect, elements could have been better planned, better executed, or both. Specifics to be examined include completeness of the handover report including identification of residual errors (bugs), adequacy of transition tools for data conversion, process conversion, error confirmation, and completion validation. The training given to both users and maintenance staff is also evaluated for content and delivery, and the adequacy of procedures supporting the new system is

assessed. Managers can comment on whether changes in responsibilities were correctly identified and implemented.

- Lessons Learned. This is a summarization and formatting of key points in the preceding discussions. A brief paragraph is adequate for each item.
- Recommendations. A further summarization of points deemed sufficiently important is to be addressed by specific recommendations. These fall into two groups: (1) actions required to maximize the success of the project and (2) global actions the Delivery Organization should implement to improve future project success.

Owner/Provider Guidance

(1) Harvesting Benefits. A weakness of most methodologies is that they omit any formalization of the assessment of benefits achievement, in most cases the entire reason for undertaking the project. The inclusion of the assessment stage in the business lifecycle is a step toward resolving this, but an explicit examination of the business benefits attained is a concern of the risk lifecycle system, described in the section *Did we benefit?* It is entirely an owner's preoccupation and therefore not a subject for collaboration. Nonetheless, any manager concerned about formalizing the methods for defining and achieving benefits and creating business awareness in project management should examine the approach described in *The Information Paradox: Realizing the Business Benefits of Information Technology.*[1]

Client/Vendor Guidance

(1) Exceptions. As with all elements in this guide, joint completion of activities is prescribed in the belief this generates superior results. This is the focus of the Delivery Organization. I recognize this is not always possible, or even desirable in a client/vendor situation, specifically in the following cases: assessment of financial results, evaluation of personnel, and development of lessons learned. The parties can agree to undertake these reviews within their own organizations.

(2) Warranty. This is almost certain to be a contractual obligation and is part of the post-handover picture. During this period, clients need assurances they are not being abandoned and extra effort should be made to ensure the enabling procedures are working smoothly. Concurrently, the vendor is usually interested in establishing a maintenance contract to take over when warranty ends.

(3) Assessment Funding. Although clients should be encouraged to formalize the assessment stage and prepare an assessment report, it is unlikely this would be included in the contract. The vendor should review with the client the most useful role and scope of vendor involvement in this stage and provide funding through a change request.

Summary of Delivery Organization Elements

This account of DO element details has familiarized the reader with the workings of 22 DO elements and the joint responsibilities of owner/provider. The elements themselves (with a few exceptions) are not innovations or unknown to most PMs. The innovation is in pre-specifying and agreeing with these elements *at the beginning* of a project with the intent of engaging *jointly* in their application or development. Thus, although the number of items might seem large, they are not representative of extra effort, and they simply repackage work to be done in any case. The DO method, however, results in less friction, probably less work, and much better outcomes.

It helps to place these elements back into context by concluding with the summarization shown in Table 3.1. For each of the 22 elements listed by stage, reference code, and name, the table lists each of the following attributes:

Definition of Delivery Organization Element Attributes

- Purpose: More clarity behind the reason for implementing the element, or the condition being promoted.
- Responsibility: Who among the project principles is *primarily* responsible to execute the element or alternatively gain agreement for its exclusion?
- Beneficial User: Who is likely to be the most important user of the element result? This is sometimes the same as the person with responsibility.
- Key Value: Execution of the element may involve a process, a specialized technique, a review session, and a resulting document (or update). Quite often, two or three of these activities are involved. But the true value of the element usually centers on one, which is where the best effort should be applied.
- Annotated with C for Core: This is not meant to imply the other elements are therefore unimportant, but when certain criteria are considered (e.g., small project) they may be considered optional.

Table 3.1

Attributes of Delivery Organization elements

REF	NAME	PURPOSE	RESPONSIBILITY	BENEFICIAL USER	KEY VALUE	C-CORE
INITIATION STAGE						
DO1	Project Charter	Mandate	Sponsor	Project Mgr	Document	C
DO2	Joint Mgt Agreements	Consensus	Project Mgr	All	Process	
DO3	Lifecycle Walkthrough	Understanding	Project Mgr	Project Mgr	Review	
DO4	Lifecycle Mapping	Accountability	Project Mgr	All	Technique	
DO5	Project Risk Register	Delivery	Project Mgr	Sponsor	Document	C
DO6	Risk Factor Checklist	Delivery	Project Mgr	Sponsor	Technique	
DO7	RAM	Accountability	Project Mgr	Project Mgr	Technique	
DO8	Initiation Checklist	Control	Delivery Mgr	All	Review	C
EXECUTION STAGE						
DO9	Project Status Report	Information	Project Mgr	Sponsor	Document	C
DO10	Risk Alert Checklist	Delivery	Project Mgr	All	Review	C
DO11	Change Management	Control	Project Mgr	All	Process	C
DO12	Issue Management	Control	Project Mgr	All	Process	C
DO13	Decision Requests	Accountability	Project Mgr	Project Mgr	Process	
DO14	Deliverable Acceptance	Delivery	Owner	All	Process	
DO15	Phase End Report	Information	Project Mgr	Sponsor	Document	
DO16	Dashboard Report	Information	Delivery Mgr	Provider	Document	
COMPLETION STAGE						
DO17	Project Sign-off	Delivery	Sponsor	Project Mgr	Document	C
DO18	Transition Plan	Delivery	Owner	All	Document	
DO19	Completion Checklist	Control	Delivery Mgr	All	Review	C
ASSESSMENT STAGE						
DO20	Satisfaction Survey	Information	Owner	All	Review	
DO21	Performance Evaluation	Improvement	Resource Mgr	Team	Review	
DO22	Assessment Report	Improvement	Delivery Mgr	All	Process	C

Note

1 Thorp, John. 1999. *The Information Paradox: Realizing the Business Benefits of Information Technology*, McGraw-Hill.

4 Shared Collaborative Practices

The 22 elements just discussed require no special skill to execute, just a basic understanding of the management process, though some may be facilitated by a professional familiar with risk practice. They are the tools needed to organize and administrate the project, or at least the tools requiring the collaboration of stakeholders. It is the job of the DO to ensure all stakeholders are familiar with these tools, and importantly, expect to see them in use when they are engaged in a project.

Before investigating how these elements operate and the best way to implement the Delivery Organization, I want to move away from the detail of the previous chapter and outline how collaboration can play a role in some of the more specialized or professional practices. These may be considered shared practices. For completeness, I have also included the following chapter which overviews independent practices, that is, practices adopted by either the provider or owner and implemented independently without requiring collaboration to be fully effective.

Much of what follows draws on standard project management practice but is adapted to the requirements of collaboration, business, and delivery management.

Collaborative practices can be used on projects, but to succeed they must be properly supported and formally applied. There must also be a fair degree of trust between the parties. Based on my experience, collaboration benefits arise from these *best project practices:*

(1) Organizational Accountability
(2) Risk Management
(3) Quality Management
(4) Resource Management

The focus of this chapter is applying these practices in a collaborative owner/provider setting and presenting the supporting techniques. This includes

DOI: 10.4324/9781003370031-5

more information on seven of the DO elements drawn from three of these practices, namely, DO4, DO5, DO6, DO7, DO10, DO14, and DO17.

This chapter provides a comprehensive description of how the owner and provider work together to solve problems usually addressed by the provider working in isolation. Traditionally, the client has determined that because the project is now in the hands of a project team, matters of risk, quality, accountability, and resource management are for the PM to resolve. For their part, the project team has discovered the reluctance of the owner to engage and has retreated into their own project silo. The work may be getting done, but the perspective lacks the contribution of the owner, who is paying the bill. The Delivery Organization commits to a collaborative approach and transforms the role of the provider from isolated doer to facilitator and solution advisor.

Organizational Accountability

One of the areas for improvement in the organization of project teams is ensuring accountability for work is responsibly assigned and understood. In project recovery reviews, I have frequently found that an inadequate definition of responsibilities was a cause of failure. To recap, I have already discussed ways and means of responding to this inadequacy. The section *Owner/Provider Balance* looked at harnessing the natural interests and tension between provider and acceptor to formalize acceptance responsibilities. Additionally, the lifecycle mapping and RAM techniques were described and endorsed. The result was the specification of four accountability techniques within the required DO elements:

(1) DO4 Lifecycle Mapping clarifies the deliverable responsibilities when multiple PMs are involved, such as a business and technical PM, or several contracted provider PMs.
(2) DO7 Responsibility Assignment Matrix (RAM) is a useful element to allocate responsibility for deliverables or activities among managers, teams, and stakeholders.
(3) DO14 Deliverable Acceptance element documents the completion of a transaction between provider and owner.
(4) DO17 Project Sign-off is a specialized element documenting the completion of the project.

In this section, I present additional frameworks to support the assignment of responsibility and accountability among the project team and stakeholders. These are the Responsibility, Accountability, and Authority (RAA) model and the structure chosen for the project team itself.

Responsibility, Accountability, and Authority (RAA)

Ambiguous, ill-defined, incomplete, or ignored stakeholder responsibilities often imperil project success. A useful model to highlight how this failure can be avoided is the triplet of RAA. This is often drawn as a three-legged stool, shown in Figure 4.1, suggesting if one leg is removed the stool falls over.

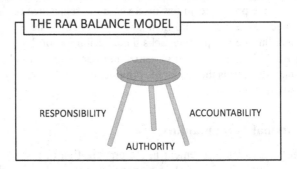

Figure 4.1 The RAA balance model

Source: First published in Commercial Project Management, 2017

Responsibility is what you have agreed to do or are professionally expected to do as a duty. If you are responsible, then you must execute tasks over which you have control, based on the level and nature of the responsibility.

Accountability is the other side of responsibility. If an assigned or implied responsibility is accepted, then you are accountable for the proper discharge of the responsibility and can be held accountable for the associated success measure. This is a fundamental and sometimes neglected principle of management. Holding people accountable requires all parameters of the responsibility must be spelled out or professionally implied and there are consequences if they are not met.

Responsibility can be segmented and delegated quite precisely and may then be measured by task performance rather than overall success or failure. Accountability implies a consequence resulting from poor performance, or failure, and can never be totally delegated. Accountability flows down the chain of command, but success measures become progressively narrower because accountabilities can never be 100% delegated.

Authority, like accountability, flows down in an organization. Authority is a mandate, a freedom of action. The greater the authority, the more freedom enjoyed. Freedom means the license to incur costs, to issue commands, to hire and fire, to present issues and solutions, and to make decisions – all on one's own account. This is the most difficult of our triplet to deal with because project management principles require authority to be clear and explicit, whereas general management is more comfortable with an element of ambiguity.

People can be held accountable for the performance of their assigned responsibilities but only for the broader success of the project in line with an increase in their authority. Thus, the authority of PMs must be in balance with their accountability for success. Whatever the degree of delegation, adequate authority must be granted – greater accountability requires more authority.

Collaborative assignment of responsibilities for a project requires a full set of project management responsibilities to be defined, consistent with the goal to deliver the project on schedule, on budget, and meeting agreed objectives. Table 4.1 provides a complete checklist. Best practice is to check these responsibilities at the start of the project and confirm those delegated to the PM and those residing with provider or owner management.

Clear and agreed allocation of responsibilities is an excellent first step, and essential if senior management is to fulfil its role of holding project principals accountable. It falls primarily to the delivery manager and the sponsor, each from their own perspective, to ensure the global spectrum of accountability is properly enforced.

The main concern of the PMs, once their accountability is established, is to ensure their authority is adequate. This is discussed and confirmed with the delivery manager and the sponsor during initiation. Not all of this is feasible to record, but the essentials must end up in the project charter, contract, initiation checklist, or equivalent document. A complete checklist of possible authorities is shown in Table 4.2. An important check is to ensure

Table 4.1

Project Manager Responsibility Checklist	
Plan the project, establish, and maintain project objectives, scope, and quality	Monitor progress and report status (schedule, budget, scope)
Manage the expectations of sponsor and steering committee	Detect variances (schedule, budget, scope) and take action
Design the project approach	Assess risk and take mitigating action
Prepare plans and budgets	Manage changes
Acquire resources, ensure staff orientation	Resolve issues, escalating as necessary
Organize teams, resources, procedures, etc.	Monitor and coach team performance
Obtain commitments	Enforce standards
Assign and supervise tasks	Feedback on team performance.

Table 4.2

Project Manager Authority Checklist	
Limit of authority for project expenses and costs	Task assignment
Limit of authority for project change requests	Implementation of risk mitigation
Hiring of staff or contractors	Scope of decision-making and issue resolution
Staff re-assignment	Access to information
Staff development	Access to senior staff
Staff recognition	Modification of standards or operating procedures
Use of contingency or reserves	Management of performance

rough equivalence of authority, or delegation limits, between comparable owner/provider managers. This contributes to a more efficient execution environment.

PM's can strengthen their position by using the RAA model in discussions. It is essential to avoid accepting responsibility and accountability for which adequate authority has not been given. In fact, everyone should check for this balance too, before accepting a project role.

Thus, the RAA model provides an excellent means to ensure proper functioning within the project structure. But what about the project structure itself? Different structures may be applied to different projects, and this clearly influences responsibilities and accountabilities.

Project Structure and Accountability

In the discussion on the silo effect, I noted the inefficiencies caused by constant referrals up the command structure when requests, decisions, or issues were in play. In commercial scenarios, this inefficiency may be compounded by contract referrals. Is it possible to create a project structure both efficient and maintaining clear divisions of accountability?

There are three basic project structures the Delivery Organization must consider, illustrated in Figure 4.2. Effort should be made to agree with a project structure during project materialization, as it provides a framework for the detailing of responsibilities during initiation. The project structure should not be decreed unilaterally, as the provider and owner may have valid and competing interests. Each of the three options has strengths and weaknesses, and naturally there are also hybrid solutions possible.

(1) Parallel Teams. This structure is not particularly integrated but is popular and easy to implement. The project manager commands the

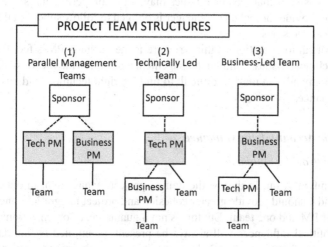

Figure 4.2 Project team structures

provider team (technical), and an owner-manager commands the owner team (business). There is freedom on both sides to design the reporting details to suit their own needs. Both managers must sort through their own deliverables and task responsibilities, integrated into the Delivery Organization with use of DO4 Mapping.

The drawback to this arrangement is the difficulty of integration. Joint team operations are made more complex by the separate reporting lines. If there are multiple owner departments involved, a common point of project authority may only be reached by the sponsor.

(2) Provider (Technically) Led Team. Giving the lead to the provider PM is almost always the 'get it done' option. This is the way to go if time is of the essence. The PM understands the nature and complexity of what is being built, and the methods, tools, techniques to build it, but may not be in tune with business requirements and priorities.

This structure has some strength. The PM understands the technical opportunities and limitations, reports to the sponsor, and represents an integrated provider and owner team. This, plus an effective relationship with the sponsor (key decision-maker), should ensure responsive action and efficient project execution.

(3) Owner (Business) Led Team. This solution is chosen when the owner wants maximum assurance the best possible product will be delivered, in terms of meeting the needs of the business. Paradoxically, this arrangement usually distances the sponsor from the project, who may feel comfortable delegating more to the business-oriented PM. The

downside is that technical issues may not be properly understood, and the provider or technical manager is obliged to follow suboptimal technical decisions.

Critical to operation of this structure is the business PM's feel for the technical issues. Unified management control, with the business in command, can make it difficult to find the right technical and business balance.

Specific Accountability Guidance

Owner/Provider Guidance

(1) Unified Team. In theory, the unified project management in options 2 and 3 should provide greater cohesion and project integration: one senior PM and one team. But this is not a guarantee, as organizational and political influences will always be present, as implied by the dashed lines in the charts. Nonetheless, an administratively unified team ensures collective adoption of collaborative DO elements and, especially with business leadership, easier uptake with all other stakeholders.

(2) Technical PM. Occasionally, under option 2, a Business PM may not be appointed which allows the Technical PM to presume a wider responsibility and an opportunity to build a cohesive team. But this carries some risk as it places greater demands on the Technical PM. Under option 3, it is almost certain a subordinate Technical PM will be appointed because a Business PM does not possess the needed technical knowledge.

(3) Acceptance Authority. If option 2 or 3 is successfully implemented giving the prospect of a solid, integrated team, another possible risk can arise. The integration of a provider and owner team tends to weaken the deliverable and system acceptance model described in *Owner/Provider Balance*. For this reason, the sponsor may choose to appoint the system manager, or eventual hands-on owner of the system, as the acceptance authority.

(4) Conclusion. All other matters being equal, the following guidance is valid:

- Parallel management teams are easy to assemble and the best option when team integration is less essential.
- When business needs and wants are paramount, use a business-led team.
- When results are needed quickly, use a technically led team.

Client/Vendor Guidance

(1) Decision-making. In option 1, although the vendor PM's influence with the sponsor must be earned, usually the vendor PM will enjoy considerable authority to keep things moving. In the event of conflicting objectives not easily resolved between the vendor PM and the business manager, access to the sponsor allows both to make their case and the decision made.

(2) Technical Authority. Even when option 2 offers a superior solution given the demands of the project, clients are often unwilling to hand this degree of authority to a vendor. This is further complicated when a technical team from the client is also required for the project. Reporting them to the vendor technical manager allows for excellent coordination and response to priorities but meets with client reluctance. Trust and openness are essential. Depending on the degree of team integration, and the unpredictability of workload in this environment, it may also be challenging to design a workable fixed-price contract. Usually, Time and Material (T&M) might be preferred. Alternatively, a hybrid approach can be adopted with some management staff on T&M and selected deliverables agreed on a Fixed-Price (FP) basis.

(3) Delivery Authority. If option 3 is implemented, then the vendor PM reports to a client business manager. In this scenario, the vendor must look carefully at contractual commitments to ensure they have adequate authority to deliver.

Risk Management

Risk pervades our lives, shapes our strategies, and influences our behavior. I am convinced expertise in risk management should be a priority for every PM, right after mastering the triple constraint. Risk fluency allows the PM to depersonalize risk scenarios, so rather than negative accusations the discussion centers on the risks and what should be done about them. This makes the PM's job more productive, improves the project's chance of success, and offers a good payback for the analysis effort required.

In this section, I summarize the risk models thoroughly described in the reference *Commercial Project Management*[1] and demonstrate how they can be used as in-house collaborative tools for project risk management. These models describe a global perspective of project risk recommended for senior managers, and detailed models to help PMs with planning and execution risk. Risk techniques form a central platform of the Delivery Organization and make up three required elements of the DO:

(1) DO5 Project Risk Register identifies specific risk events and documents a risk response.
(2) DO6 Risk Factor Checklist uses a set of intrinsic risk factors in the environment, assembled from experience of previous projects, to provide a planning framework used to rank the assessed project risk and to suggest mitigations.
(3) DO10 Risk Alert Checklist identifies leading indicators or 'telltales' of looming project trouble in the four standard chains of project performance. The checklist consolidates these results and issues an overall management alert assessed as red, yellow, or green.

Systems Approach to Risk

In my experience, the standalone risk event model universally used by PMs does not provide enough structure and support to reliably manage lifecycle risk. It needs to be supplemented by a systems approach which aligns risk with the unique factors of each delivery stage. This method of project risk management is particularly useful because, as shown in Figure 4.3, it maps to the business lifecycle which is the foundation of the Delivery Organization. It shows how project risk naturally evolves through the lifecycle and the changing risk assessment questions to be asked. As risk changes in nature, so too does the affected party, suggesting 'ownership' of risk can migrate. This provides a naturally collaborative framework and produces better management results than the classic approach which concentrates all the analysis, responsibility, and mitigation on the PM.

The model shows that there is more to this than listing risks and delegating the PM to get on with it. There are at least three key stakeholder groups who 'own' varying elements of risk:

Risk Owners

(1) The Owner (sponsor) is primarily responsible for project selection and benefits management. This responsibility may be clearly personified in the sponsor or may be split between subordinates.
(2) The Provider is responsible for giving advice on technical viability, execution proposals, project policies, risk-based portfolio management, resourcing and hiring practices, Standard Operating Procedures (SOP) and methodology, setting and maintaining performance standards, and overall owner(s) satisfaction.

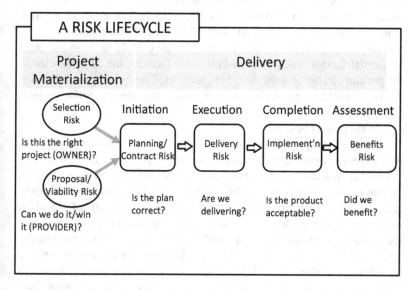

Figure 4.3 A risk lifecycle

(3) The project manager is responsible for project risk mitigation in response to the question "what might prevent the work I am authorizing from meeting the project objectives?" Based on project size and complexity, elements of this question can in turn be delegated to team managers.

As the project moves through each stage of the lifecycle, the stage of risk naturally evolves in step. Each stage can be investigated in terms of a representative risk question, its ownership, and the political pressures that naturally intervene. This model and the associated techniques help support the collaborative approach to risk minimization.

Materialization Stage

There are two questions characterizing *selection and viability risk* during the materialization stage.

Is this the right project?

Projects need a verifiable reason for their existence. This may be an essential requirement such as a government regulation change, a response to the marketplace, a cost-saving initiative, or a competitive cost/benefit analysis. Usually, there is insufficient funding for all feasible projects and these factors need to be analyzed to eliminate the less essential projects from the annual plan. This question clearly belongs to the owner.

Comparing competitive projects may require tools to examine other influential factors. Such tools include brainstorming, the decision matrix, the pro and con list, and the force field analysis. Employing a neutral skilled facilitator will help get the best solution when there are competing projects and owners.

Can the project be done?

This is primarily a question of feasibility and should assess several factors including owner and provider team, degree of technical innovation or unfamiliarity, and reliability of size and duration estimates. These questions belong to both owner and provider and because they involve uncertainly, rarely result in a yes or no answer but are expressed in terms of probabilities. A familiar example involves an owner demanding a tight deadline. Can the provider really stand up and clearly state it can't be done? Very rarely, and if you do, you risk your job! In these situations, we are dealing with the uncertainty of estimates, and the estimate is viewed as inferior if it doesn't meet the owner's needs. In such cases, a risk-based collaboration might lead to a conclusion both parties can live with.

Tools for preliminary risk identification are suitable for this question, including the fishbone diagram and a standard risk screener. At this early stage, it is helpful to pre-populate the fishbone diagram with at least five 'ribs' – environment, methods, people, technology, and materials. The analysis requires owner and provider collaboration.

Initiation Stage

There is one primary question to interrogate *planning risk* during the initiation stage, though there maybe a few supplementary questions that follow naturally.

Is the plan correct?

Other questions might concern the identification of stakeholders, the project organization, and level of executive support and approval. Initiation is a transition stage from the sponsor, who has been the prime motivator, to the newly appointed PM who is establishing the leadership role. Both will have a keen interest in risk identification and management, but the PM has a more visceral connection. The PM must pick up on commitments and assumptions made by superiors and develop a clear understanding. There may be a preliminary project plan which the PM inherits along with the expectations it has established. Initiation is the last opportunity to develop a realistic baseline to govern the execution of the project. In response to this need, the Delivery Organization specifies a standardized approach using both the risk event model and a systemized risk planning model.

The Risk Event Model

The classic risk event model is ubiquitous and leads directly to development of the DO5 Risk Register.

The risk event model in Figure 4.4 is based on cause-and-effect analysis and requires the analyst to examine the project asking, "what could go wrong?" and "what is the cause?" With those questions answered, it is then possible to either eliminate or deflect the cause, or minimize the impact if the event occurs. In risk parlance, this is called the response strategy. Although centered on mitigation, there are three other strategies identified – transference, avoidance, and acceptance.

Success with this model relies on adequate root cause analysis. Like the traditional Russian doll where layers are opened until the final layer is discovered, the root cause must be revealed. A useful technique is to express root cause analysis in terms of a semantic model that, if properly done, immediately suggests mitigation.

"Because <of cause> then <risk event> may occur {repeat to root cause}, causing <impact on project objectives>"

A simple example might be: "Because of a very competitive marketplace then loss of a key resource may occur, causing delay to project schedule". Phrased this way, reasonably effective mitigations can be designed.

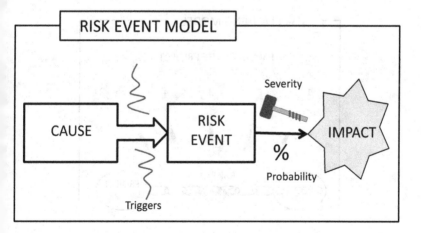

Figure 4.4 The risk event model

Source: First published in Commercial Project Management, 2017

The Risk Planning Model

The risk planning model shown in Figure 4.5 is based on the concept of many *risk factors* prevalent in the project environment, each having a cumulative effect on the project. This complements but contrasts with the *risk event/risk register* approach which is focused on high-impact one-time possibilities and often involves guesswork. A failure may arise from occurrence of a risk event but can also result from what might be termed 'death by a thousand cuts'. In this view, risk is also an environmental factor and can be planned for by analysis rather than guesswork about the future. Building the model requires some development effort and access to project experience, but the payback is risk management for projects which becomes more reliable and much easier.

The model presupposes that success means the project work results in the achievement of project objectives. Risk is the uncertainty of meeting those objectives and uses the metaphor of daggers portraying *risk factors* continually attacking the binding links. These are not unforeseen 'bolts from the blue' but can be predefined by analysis. Risk factors are deemed to lurk in the universal *facets* of the project class, based on the nature of the application and implementation environment. A risk facet is usually generic, such as project properties, of which size is a factor (large is higher risk than small), and duration and deadlines are others (a flexible schedule is lower risk, a long inflexible schedule is high). Some facets might derive from the relationship between the owner and provider organizations, such as contractual terms. Others might be specific to the application area – in software development one facet is the business solution, an example of a factor being clarity of requirements.

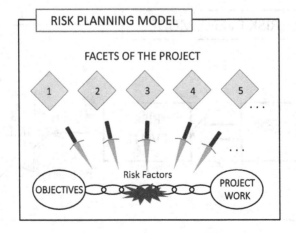

Figure 4.5 The risk planning model

Source: First published in Commercial Project Management, 2017

This model is usually enhanced using numerical methods to determine a comparative *risk rank* for the project. Risk rank can be used by senior management for portfolio management and to assess the degree of reporting and audit required. The resulting risk tool can easily be adapted for collaborative use by provider and owner to codify management's response based on the risk rank and to identify additional mitigations. The model also establishes a conceptual base for the subsequent execution risk model.

Mitigations uncovered by the risk event model and risk planning model are then built into the project plan to be baselined.

Execution Stage

There is one dominant question to address *delivery risk* during the execution stage.

Are we delivering?

Risk assessment must undergo a shift in thinking as a project enters execution. This mirrors the character of the project itself. During the planning, everything is future and speculative. Now, the project has started and the 'real issues' of the project can be experienced and observed. This calls for a supplementary approach to the future-focused risk register and is based on a risk execution model. The result of this analysis is the DO10 Risk Alert Checklist and is the responsibility of the PM.

The Risk Execution Model

As already expressed in the planning model, success is defined by the project work achieving all project objectives and risk is the uncertainty of meeting those objectives. To assess risk faced by an executing project, we expand the chain binding work and objectives into multiple chains each representing an observable aspect of project performance. These *performance chains* are then conceived as a series of links of *risk alerts* measurable during project execution and indicative of the project's overall risk to achieve objectives. This is illustrated in Figure 4.6.

A performance chain reflects the progress of the project toward the achievement of one or more objectives, so there could be as many performance chains as there are objectives. An obvious example is the financial performance chain. After identifying each performance chain for the project, the risk alerts can be defined. For example, a link in the financial chain might be the amount of internal contingency consumed.

Using predefined risk alerts for the designated performance chains, a checklist can be set up at the beginning of a project and assessed by the PM on a regular reporting cycle. The status of the alerts, consolidated into

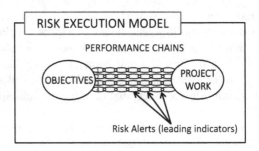

Figure 4.6 The risk execution model

Source: First published in Commercial Project Management, 2017

the performance chain, can then be summarized as a composite *risk alert* characterizing the overall execution risk of the project. This is commonly coded as red, yellow, or green (RYG), and after joint review by the owner and provider can be used to trigger the protocol for management support, intervention, or project restructuring.

The standard performance chains, applicable to all projects, are delivery, financial, team efficiency, and owner/provider relationship. These chains can be expanded to include the owner's detailed view of the project objectives. Table 4.3 shows a list of sample client objectives that could be added, though they are obviously specific to the project. Alerts (which are sometimes intuitive) are identified for each custom objective.

The state of each chain is then characterized by rating the risk alerts on the DO10 Risk Alert Checklist, which yields a composite RYG alert. The DO specifies the response protocol, based on the value of the project alert. This checklist is a key element for use by the DO to assess delivery during execution.

Completion Stage

There is a fundamental and sometimes difficult question at the core of the *implementation risk* during the completion stage.

Is the product acceptable?

The risk of this question can only be resolved by thorough acceptance testing. The description of the completion stage in *Stages of the Business Lifecycle* explains a controlled way to achieve project sign-off by writing and executing a completion mini-plan agreed upon by owner and provider. A significant part of this plan involves formal acceptance activities.

Table 4.3

Listing of Client Objectives

OBJECTIVE	DESCRIPTION
1 Business specific	The project may have some very precise business objectives that derive from the overall goal. For example, to reduce departmental costs by 10%
2 Functionality	A high-level statement of the functional requirements for the project, as this is closely linked to project scope
3 Cost	The customer's cost will include their own variable costs and fixed costs such as the contracted fixed-price project
4 Schedule	There will be end date objectives and probably interim dates to be attained to match cyclic business events, optimize benefits, comply with regulations, link with external events, or meet internal political requirements
5 Technical	Projects may be required to implement specific technologies within the developed product
6 Performance	The product must operate within a specified performance envelope in a specified environment (speed, endurance, capacity, economy, responsiveness, and so forth)
7 Quality	Explicit quality targets may have to be met such as residual defects, MTBF, or related requirements such as ease of use, maintainability, and durability
8 Process	There may be a need to follow a specific process, for example, to ensure auditability, or to meet ISO certification
9 Standards	The project or product must comply with specified standards, for example, using templates or meeting building codes
10 Environmental	There may be an objective related to environmental issues (footprint and disturbance, resource usage, sustainability, etc.)
11 HR/Safety	Certain projects may have mandatory training requirements, safety targets, or other HR objectives

Common test practice is for the provider to execute tests under their control, often called a Factory Acceptance Test (FAT), and when completed satisfactorily the owner conducts a Site Acceptance Test (SAT). The origins of SAT were focused purely on testing site installation and interface issues unable to be simulated during FAT, but nowadays all too often the owner adopts the test suites used during FAT and repeats them, usually less skillfully. This is time-consuming and inefficient. Unless the two test teams are completely independent, which is painful, disagreements surface about who should be involved in testing and writing test specifications. A better solution is for jointly planned and fully collaborative acceptance testing. The planning for this can be started quite early, even before development begins, and should be guided by a business requirements expert and a technical test expert who understands how to assemble a demanding environment to truly stress the system. Acceptance testing is the last in a test sequence including unit, function, and integration testing. A passing grade from this means an acceptable product.

Apart from acceptance testing, there are usually peripheral deliverables that must also be accepted during completion, such as training material, maintenance documentation, selected transition activities, and so forth. With those complete, and perhaps further written assurances from the PM, it is the responsibility of the owner to approve the DO17 Project Sign-off. The sign-off authority is the sponsor, who sometimes delegates this to a subordinate.

Assessment Stage

An important, obvious, but often forgotten question must be faced to determine if *benefits risk* occurred.

Did we benefit?

Obviously, this stage is far too late in the game to first think about benefits. Benefits are a fundamental reason for undertaking the project in the first place and must be clearly articulated during project materialization. As the project proceeds, a parallel activity in the owner's organization must be devoted to ensuring benefits will be attained. This will probably not occur automatically and may require careful analysis and action to bring it about. This is where the benefits risk can truly be found and does not really lend itself to collaborative effort, belonging completely to the owner. However, note collaborative use of the DO11 Change Management element can often arise from ongoing benefits analysis.

The DO22 Assessment Report is retrospective, aimed at performance improvement for both provider and owner, though its evaluation of objectives might assist in determining if and how promised benefits failed to occur. The recommendations may offer rectification proposals, or ideas on how to avoid this in future projects as part of the corporate continuous improvement initiative.

Specific Risk Guidance

Risk, in general, and the systematic models used for collaboration are a large subject suitable for further training and analysis. In the following, I have summarized selected key points from the references for both the general owner/provider case and specifically for the client/vendor.

Owner/Provider Guidance

(1) Wrong Project. In some organizations, the PM carries accountability for the benefits and not just the deliverables of the project. This is controversial and is only workable if the PM has technical and business knowledge and is given a more influential role. In particular, engagement during feasibility and a role in decision-making helps avoid selection of the wrong project, or at least ensures a role to identify risks and mitigations arising from a poor decision.

(2) Negotiation. Speaking truth to power needs an impersonal framework, as well as guts. Risk modeling facilitates this approach, depersonalizes concerns, and deals in probabilities rather than assertions. When stakeholder preferences are contrary to project reality, or other pressures arise, the PM can use risk models to develop a more constructive discussion leading to better project outcomes. Negotiation, if needed, can secure extra funding for mitigation or contingencies, in return for a properly anchored project commitment and increased probability of success.

(3) Inexperience. The risk factor approach captures previous project experience and standard mitigations to enhance the risk planning work of a less experienced PM. The risk factors can be deduced by analysis of projects in a similar class. These factors can then be modeled to determine their effect on project objectives and hence the risk rank of the project. This concept of risk as an environmental factor and planned for by analysis is also applied to execution and the development of standard risk alerts (leading indicators of trouble ahead) and a consolidated RYG project alert. These models require some development effort and access to project experience, but the payback is the systemization of risk management and its use by those with less experience to gain quick and reliable results.

(4) Risk Portfolio. Putting a reliable and consistent system in place for early assessment of risk rank facilitates overall business risk management. Using project risk rank supports the concept of a risk portfolio and is central to maintaining the cumulative risk profile of commitments at a desired level.

(5) Rank versus Alert. Risk rank is an attribute of the project assigned at the time it was planned. Its value lies in the planning context and is supplemented during execution by the risk alert. What counts is the present risk alert status and the response. The rank does not change. It is perfectly consistent for a project to be performing well (green) and be ranked as a high-risk project.

Client/Vendor Guidance

(1) Project Bids. The vendor PM is usually a junior partner in the sales effort, led by a sales executive who will wisely ask for the PM's assessment of the bid opportunity. The PM's efforts are directed toward the estimates, the delivery risks, and ensuring price negotiations don't lead to cuts in the proposed project team. In the absence of an appointed PM, this role is performed by the delivery manager.

(2) Contract Risk. A balanced contract requires engagement of the PM and authority to ensure contract commitments for the project are attainable. The PM should be on a par with the sales executive, who nonetheless remains accountable until the contract is signed. In the absence of an appointed PM, this role is performed by the delivery manager. The contract effectively replaces the project charter in determining the PM mandate.

(3) Risk Perspective. Although the project benefits from a joint approach by owner/provider to risk management during planning and execution, there are obviously differences of viewpoint in the commercial environment. The vendor must exercise situational judgment when sharing business information. Usually, unique vendor risks are assessed and managed internally.

Quality Management

Only a few quality elements are featured in the 22 DO elements. Those chosen strongly support a collaborative approach and can be understood and acted on by a non-expert. In other words, training needs are minimal. The two quality elements that meet these criteria are usually part of conventional QA/QC practice:

- DO14 Deliverable Acceptance documents the completion of a transaction between provider and owner (shared with accountability practice).
- DO17 Project Sign-off is a specialized form of transaction completion that documents the completion of the project (shared with accountability practice).

Now we are considering additional elements taken from quality management as a specific practice, to implement a complete quality system. Regrettably, the fundamentals of project quality – planning and executing a project that meets clearly agreed quality requirements – involve specialized project activities that even experts have difficulty defining.

I have contemplated this issue over the latter half of my career and developed models and techniques to make quality management more meaningful.

Communicating quality requirements and quality results between owner and provider has always been challenging, so there is a real need for collaborative quality tools, and these I describe in this section. They are not suitable for beginner implementation and my purpose is to offer these new ideas primarily to a provider who is already working with the owner on project quality. These ideas are:

- A Basic Definition of Project Quality
- Four Models of Project Quality
- A Quality Environment.

It is possible your organization has implemented one of several corporate quality environments (e.g., ISO9000, SEI Capability Maturity Model, Total Quality Management, Quality Function Deployment, or Six Sigma) in which case it must be properly integrated with the Delivery Organization. But there is still value in the following recommendations because your corporate quality initiative may not target project quality specifics, neither are they covered in PMBOK®, PRINCE2®, or Lean.

A Fresh View of Quality Definitions
Quality is not a sprinkle of fairy dust.

Classical quality practices such as quality assurance and control have emphasized procedures for defect prevention, detection, and removal, as well as hygienic factors such as adherence to standards, methodology, and audits. These may be necessary but have given rise to the impression quality is something that can be 'added on'. The endgame, namely both a product meeting functional and quality specifications, and the correctness of activities to build it, requires quality to be defined and managed as an *inherent* part of the project itself. These two aspects of quality, product and project quality, require fresh definitions contrived to recognize their natural, intrinsic place in the project.

Product Quality means the product possesses discernable, tangible, and measurable quality factors. As a simple example of how quality factors are developed from subjective needs, let's assume the client wants a 'robust' system. Discussion establishes reliability as a quality objective. Using one of the techniques, we work with the client to quantify this objective in terms of Mean Time Between Failure (MTBF). Experts from the project team establish the quality factors to achieve this objective. One factor is the need for specific critical components to be redundant. Thus:

> *Product Quality is the degree to which quality factors that serve objectives are incorporated into the product.*

Intrinsic *Project Quality* means the activities to design and implement the product quality factors are consciously included, and these activities are done well. A colloquial expression might be 'doing the right thing and doing it right'. Project quality ensures product quality is coming into being and activities are being performed to a specified standard. The feedback is immediate – no waiting for the test phase. Changes are naturally controllable through the normal change control system. And there are no out-of-the-ordinary expenses being added to existing project costs. Thus:

> *Project Quality is the degree to which activities efficiently create the product quality factors.*

So, activities must be correctly specified and done well. But what about features, customer appeal, value for money, exceeding expectations, and all the other complicated, multi-dimensional subjective stuff we have been told means quality? Though I contend much of this is something other than product quality, there is an evident need for the product to meet general customer requirements. That can be addressed by a reference to Deming's 'fit for purpose' quality goal, or perhaps Juran's more demonstrable version, 'fit for use'. A thorough discussion of these and other classic quality approaches can be found in *Project Management: A Systems Approach.*[2]

A Workable Project Framework

This is a back-to-basics analysis, so the best approach is to first re-establish a basic project framework, one that captures the essence of a project. Then the PM's job during project design is to ensure the project framework carries the attributes of project quality and will meet product quality objectives.

The framework I am proposing in Figure 4.7 is an adaptation of the triple constraint, substituting and expanding scope with objectives, deliverables, and activities. Trade-offs are added explicitly to the framework, to keep the model in balance with time and cost constraints and prevent uninhibited scope demands.

Does this represent the essence of projects? Well, a good test is to ask the analyst's three favorite questions: Why? What? How? The generic answer from most experienced PMs would be something like *The project is established to meet objectives (why) through the development of deliverables (what) created by the activity of the team (how)*. This statement clearly identifies the significance of objectives, deliverables, and activities. If these are our project essentials, possessing a naturalness of belonging, then we can conclude project quality is achieved when each element possesses the attributes of quality – and is complete and correct. How is this to be done?

The intention is to move away from reliance on add-on processes which attempt to create quality retrospectively. Our approach is to make a singular effort to identify tangible product quality factors the owner agrees mean quality and to use the four new elements of the project framework to ensure accurate execution. Thus:

Using the Project Model

(1) Identify Objectives. The specification of project objectives, and especially product quality objectives, is a foundation for quality results.

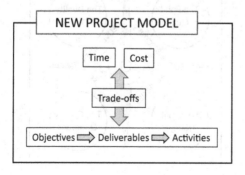

Figure 4.7 New project model

They must be tangible and support the owner's goal. There is a tendency to specify in subjective terms, and thus a need for good analytic tools (addressed in the next section) to help the provider develop a set of relevant product quality factors.

(2) Define Deliverables. Quality depends on completeness and understanding of each deliverable's purpose and how it supports the objectives. An equality of obligation and responsibility should be recognized by both parties for development and approval of deliverables, as outlined in Figure 2.6.

(3) Specify Activities. Quality viewed retrospectively using quality control techniques applied to 'completed' deliverables misses the value of paying more attention to efficient and effective activities to create the deliverable in the first place. The PM works directly with the team to help specify their activities and optimize execution prior to starting work.

(4) Negotiate Trade-offs. A good quality trade-off procedure is a rarity. Owners may have been indoctrinated with 'faster, cheaper, better', and see no need for trade-offs. Providers, unfortunately, adjust surreptitiously, or more likely let the situation ride until something breaks. A better result is achieved if trade-off negotiations are conducted earlier, allowing for proper, more reliable project planning.

The Four Quality Models

Each of the four new elements in the new project model can be modeled for quality as shown in Figure 4.8.

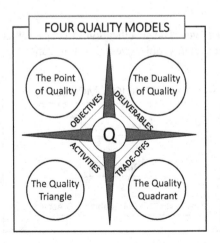

Figure 4.8 Four quality models

I have argued product quality is the aggregation of tangible quality factors possessed by the product, and project quality is an intrinsic attribute of the four elements of a project's essential framework. Quality models are offered for each of these elements, provoking techniques and methods designed to support a collaborative approach. These simple quality models have a pleasing arithmetic progression!

(1) The Point Model (The Establishment of Objectives)

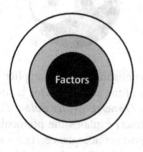

This is a logical, progressive method to achieve the cliché goal of customer satisfaction, usually only considered a retrospective response to a survey. Owners tend to consider quality primarily in subjective terms, so the PM uses the point model to ensure a shift from subjective to objective. Even this is an incomplete transition; objectives are usually only demonstrated when the product is largely finished, by which time it is too late. The model therefore requires a further decomposition of objectives into tangible product *quality factors*.

A product quality factor is defined as an observable feature of product design that promotes a desired quality objective. A technique to design these factors is based on the Socratic Q&A method bringing technical experts and owners together to collaborate over a general-purpose standard question set:

- What are your quality goals for the product? This yields a list of largely subjective needs.
- How will you know if your quality goals are met? This creates a list of quality objectives.
- What product feature would contribute to each of these objectives? This is the result of the exercise, a list of definable quality factors to be built into the product.

Detailed questions can also be prepared to drive out quality factors to meet common specifics, such as system life, durability requirements, error tolerance, conformance to commercial or technical standards, ease of usage, ease of maintenance, adaptability, expandability, and so forth.

(2) The Duality Model (Balancing the Deliverables)

In the duality model, the obligations of the supplier are recognized and balanced by the obligations of the acceptor. This is such an important part of collaboration, the section *Owner/Provider Balance* is devoted to the details. A good charter (or contract) explains the protocols for a balanced transaction, especially final product acceptance. The contract also lays out the terms of the acceptance criteria, if not the specific details. A good development methodology with built-in quality also applies the duality model to interim project deliverables, such as specifications, designs, technical plans, components, and subassemblies.

The model can be applied to many other transactions to improve quality. Examples include acknowledgment of messages, validation of requests received, and protocols governing the provision of data, materials, or resources.

(3) The Triangle Model (Efficiency of Activities)

The third model is really at the heart of quality project work assignments. Processes dominate most classic thinking on quality of work and belong in this model, but with more besides.

The quality triangle is an illustration of the three fundamentals used to create a quality activity: People, Process, and Technology (PPT). The PM uses the triangle model to optimize project activities developed in collaboration with the assigned resource.

People assignments require the PM to consider the three main attributes: experience and track record, training requirements, and behavioral and personal characteristics.

Processes cover the steps followed by the team to develop, verify, validate, and approve deliverables. Management processes (additional to team activities) may also be specified by the organization such as QA/QC, hiring, performance management, or contractual procedures.

Technology is often acquired for use by the team based on a cost/benefit justification. Such procurements should be integrated with the project activities and the budgets managed. Social media platforms such as Facebook, Twitter, and Slack should be assessed as aids to communication and coordination, as well as technology choices for document creation, modeling, CAD, methodology support, testing, requirements traceability, and version management.

(4) The Quadrant Model (Effectiveness of Trade-offs)

If schedule and budget allocations are exceeded, trade-offs must be designed to explicitly reduce work to meet the constraint. The quadrant model provides a collaborative framework for the owner and the PM to effectively negotiate changes designed to keep the project work and available resources in balance. Resources are on one axis as cost and schedule; work is represented on the second axis by product functionality and quality factors. A change in one quadrant inevitably causes a change in another.

Other techniques such as alternatives analysis and contingency assessment can also assist with the negotiation. The desired outcome is a quality specification consistent with schedule and cost constraints. Remember, though, downgrading of quality factors, or removal of the less critical functionalities, will likely have an impact on forecast maintenance budgets.

A Quality Environment

Quality is a tough subject, and the discussion has focused on our primary topic – identifying the specifics of collaborative project quality. But how does the Delivery Organization know its quality prescriptions are being followed? How does the environment promote project quality?

In the introduction to quality, I acknowledged numerous and competing corporate quality systems. They all cost money. And the proposals put forward by the popular ISO9000 standard for a mandatory Quality Management System (QMS) can appear hard and expensive. It need not be so. Briefly, because it is wandering from our collaborative theme, I want to describe a minimum environment to ensure projects are in fact following the prescription, regardless of their definition of project quality. Described here is, in effect, a basic QMS and is the responsibility of the provider and their project management.

The model in Figure 4.9 defines responsibilities, starting with the provider organization to establish the environment, and then the PM to plan the project. The provider prepares a document clearly stating their quality policy, using language that identifies specifics. The provider is also obligated to provide quality support for projects as well. The PM is required to prepare a quality plan (as per policy) and ensure it is followed during project execution.

Basic QMS Ingredients

(1) Policy supplies the mandate and is prepared, endorsed, and distributed by executive. It goes beyond a simple statement of commitment and lays out in a few paragraphs what commitment entails. Every employee should see the impact of themselves in the policy. An ideal model for policy is the quality triangle – people, process, and technology, one paragraph for each.

(2) Support the quality activity, which remains as the provider's cost unless such overhead project costs are charged to the owner. Preparing and agreeing policy is cheap – implementation is where the costs lie. If budgets are small, support commitments may be modest (but *not* nonexistent), for example, provision of templates, standardized testing environments, and a basic one-day training course. Larger providers may commit to a senior and independent quality management group within the organization. They execute a quality support mandate for all projects in liaison with the PMs.

(3) Plan for quality using a flexible document ranging from a page or so within the overall project plan to a weighty independent report. This is the responsibility of the PM (or quality specialist on larger projects). The purpose is to describe how the project will achieve the agreed quality objectives, and might therefore present standards, techniques,

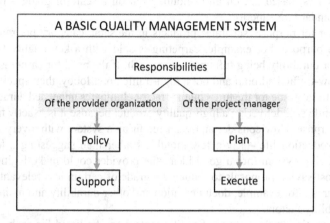

Figure 4.9 A basic quality management system

responsibilities, methods, metrics, and more. Traditional QC/QA commitments also belong here, and the content should be compliant with policy.

(4) Execute the project under the mandate of the project plan and deliver the quality requirements specified in the quality plan. Though checklists have an important role, there is no silver bullet for this component – just persistent observation, praise, and corrections as needed from the hand of the PM. Larger projects may, according to policy, warrant external quality audits, usually provided as part of the provider's support commitment.

Once the provider has figured out what quality means for their projects, a basic QMS is straightforward – develop a policy, define responsibilities for quality, build a support function, create project plans to include quality, and execute accordingly.

Specific Quality Guidance

Owner/Provider Guidance

(1) Grade. The experienced provider may wish to expand the quality requirements conversation by introducing the concept of grade. This engages Deming's notion of being fit for purpose by trading quality

factors, based not on all-or-nothing but on a scale of grade – basic, standard, or superior.

'Fit for purpose' separates products in the same category but ranging in purpose. For example, carpeting is sold with a key quality factor for durability being tufts per square inch. If the need for carpet is in a low-traffic bedroom and not a high-traffic hotel lobby, then specifying a basic grade for the tuft's quality factor eliminates unneeded durability while still delivering a high-quality product because it is exactly fit for purpose. Now consider an owner requiring a system with a very short production life – say a few months. Rather than suggesting a lower quality system (not a good idea), the provider could make legitimate cost-saving proposals to reduce the grade of certain less relevant features – for example, documentation and other durability and maintainability factors.

(2) Negotiation Preparation. Specific factors can be listed for each quadrant of the quadrant model and tabled as candidates for trade-off as shown in Table 6.5. If product quality factors were prioritized using the point model, this information now comes into play. If factors can be implemented at different grade levels, then retaining the factor at reduced grade might be an option.

Client/Vendor Guidance

(1) Default Quality. The vendor, if committed to a QMS, must ensure all project bids that include QMS activities and related project costs as part of their standard pricing model. If the client shows no inclination to specify quality, little will be gained by debate and the best approach is to proceed with the assumption of basic grade quality factors under the umbrella of the basic QMS. If the client's requirements go beyond the basic, then naturally they must be addressed by the proposal and priced accordingly. Both parties should understand the level of quality being bid before the contract is signed.

(2) ISO9000 Standard. Vendors are occasionally faced with demands from some clients for ISO9000 compliance. Without registration they will be disqualified from competitive bids. This is because the standard, which operates on a location basis, requires all contractors to be registered so the client can claim ISO9000 status for the end product. For many reasons, this standard is not always preferred by the vendor, a major impediment being the expense to obtain a rating and maintain it. A business decision must be made, and a key factor might be the volume of government business the vendor might

reasonably expect. ISO9000 has been a favorite of government and defense contractors.

Resource Management

Accountability, risk, and quality are difficult project topics, and collaboration does not always come naturally to provider and owner teams, but with perseverance the barriers to collaboration can be surmounted. The resource supply and demand practice is probably the hardest of the bunch, so there is no resource item found in the required DO elements. Despite being an important practice to get right during execution, open collaboration is tough. Why is this?

One reason is the paucity of proven and reliable management reports and methods. This leaves management uncertain, and they tend to defer difficult commitments until the last minute and beyond. There is also a feeling of defensiveness because they view their resources as their own business and nobody else. It is therefore somewhat speculative to suggest means of collaboration in this arena, but as the saying goes, nothing ventured nothing gained!

The section deals first with the basics of resource measurement and applications for reporting and responding to project resource issues. A mechanism is then proposed for collaborating on resource forecasting.

Resources and Work

Both owner and provider rely on resources of people, capital, equipment, and supplies to accomplish projects. Thus, making project commitments requires a reliable estimate of resource needs over the commitment window, and assurances those resources will be available. These estimates and assurances are inevitably tinged with uncertainty, but improvements are possible if a metrics discipline is adopted.

If you can't (or don't) measure it, you can't manage it. This well-worn maxim is a good guide to the limits of management as well as an encouragement to get out of the measuring stick. Measurements require effort but for a people-intensive service, like a system provider, they are invaluable. These metrics relate to work and to resources:

Metrics

- Work: The estimate and the actuals.
- Resources: Utilization and availability.

WORK

In our context, the work is the project, or more precisely the deliverables needed to complete the project. Work (or effort, a term used synonymously) to build the deliverables is supplied by the resources as either direct or indirect labor and is measured in units of hours. The metric has two flavors. The *estimate* calculated by the provider is the number of total hours needed to complete the project. The *actuals* are the total number of hours actually expended during execution to complete the project. The units of both these measurements are usually recorded as *work-hrs* of effort to differentiate from *hours* (or days, weeks, months) used as a unit of duration.

RESOURCES

The resource metric also has two aspects. The first is utilization, measured in work-hrs and often expressed as a percentage; the numerator is the project work-hrs devoted to the project(s) and overhead, and the denominator is the available work-hrs in the month. The second is availability, also expressed as a percentage. The numerator is the available work-hrs minus the work-hrs committed to the project(s) and overhead, and the denominator is the available work-hrs.

Utilization is a historic measure when based on actuals. It can be measured for the individual, for the project, or for the provider's resources as a whole (the business unit). If utilization uses estimates of future project work, it is sometimes referred to as expected utilization.

Categorization of utilization into different projects and types of overhead is a necessity in most time recording applications. Typical categories are project(s) work, prologue (materialization) work, general support, administration, training, vacation, and perhaps others. Resources are often engaged on more than one project, so a coding system is needed to differentiate projects and often extends to identify deliverables and activities.

The second aspect of this metric is availability, with meaning in the present or as a future estimate. It is often used as a forecast. Availability and expected utilization on all projects plus overhead will always add up to 100%. If utilization for the next month is expected to be 80%, then availability is 20%. Planned overtime pushes utilization over 100%, in which case there is no availability.

Adding the dimension of time to these metrics allows the development of *productivity* metrics, a very useful gauge for PMs but controversial because of significant variability. As an example of the results encountered, consider a resource estimated at 50% utilization for a monthly work item, but who recorded 75%. This is lower than expected productivity, but how should management respond? Was the work underestimated or the resource inefficient?

Business Unit Applications

Management of a business unit, either in-house or vendor, is not a candidate for collaborative activity, though it will be driven by reports and forecasts from the project level where collaboration is more likely. The following notes supply context, before moving to the more relevant *Project Applications*.

Resource planning is a key part of management's responsibility and success depends on reliable estimates of the planned work and the expected utilization placed on the workforce. Under-utilization is inefficient and expensive. Over-utilization means delivery targets will be missed and resources become unreliable. Annual planning sets the stage for balanced utilization during the year but remains dependent upon the forecast of workload. Resource plans are inherently variable and require monthly review and reforecast. Examples of reports to assist with business unit resource management are as follows:

- Annual Resource Plan: Utilization planned for each resource throughout the planned year.
- Monthly Planned versus Actual Utilization Report: Utilization achieved for the past month and year-to-date.
- Monthly Forecast Availability Report: Availability forecast for the coming month and balance of the year. This is the spare capacity of the business unit.

These reports enable management to take either long- or short-term response action.

Project Applications

Project managers rely on time collection and their own forecasting to develop project resource reports, determine responses to resource issues, and apply rules of thumb for quick project assessments.

Project Resource Reports

There are many reports in this category, and most are specialized using techniques such as earned value. They can be simplified into two classes of report:

(1) Actuals versus Estimate Reports. Usually listed by deliverable, these report actual hours spent compared to hours estimated. A report of

actuals to date plus estimated work-hrs to complete (Actuals + ETC) compared to work-hrs estimated (Original Estimate) is a very useful version for work in progress.

(2) Project Resource Forecast. Usually listed by resource, this reports on expected utilization over the life of the project by time period (usually monthly).

Project resource planning is a part of conventional project management. All projects, except the most trivial, have a resource plan. This is a feasible route for collaboration between owner and provider. The report usually presents the work-hrs of provider effort required per month, but its value is increased if it also includes owner resources. A simple format is shown in Table 6.6. Although provider resources are used for design and construction and are numerous, owner resources are of critical importance for certain tasks and their availability is a success factor.

Response Contingency Options

The options available to the PM depend on delegations from the provider. Otherwise, actions must be escalated to provider management. The following options assume a full delegation, and they also assume the project is attempting to match the resources to the workload and not the other way around:

(1) Hiring. If the shortfall appears sustained, then initiating the hiring process is the first option and likely requires approval for the headcount increase.

(2) Contractor. It's a good practice to maintain a relationship with external agencies. Some specialize in contracts to supply full project resources on a time and material basis and others take full project responsibility for a fixed price. This requires a procurement process, depending on policy. Other agencies specialize in selling résumés and place contracted individuals with clients for a fee. Costs are higher than an employee but having reliable resource availability in a contingency situation is reassuring.

(3) Overtime. If the over-utilization is moderate and assuredly in the short term, then overtime is a reasonable option. I would not recommend using it for a long-term solution; one reason being when the long term arrives the problem always seems to have worsened. And you can't solve the problem with overtime because you are already using it!

(4) Forced Overhead Reduction. Easy targets are vacation, time allocated to training and to unspecified general support. This route should not be taken unilaterally but negotiated with the employee.

(5) Network Outreach. This requires keeping in touch with known individuals who have traits fitting with the organization. These are trustworthy people who respect confidential situations and might consider openings as an employee or contractor, or might provide valid referrals.

Rule of Thumb (ROT)

Every experienced PM has developed personal ROTs to quickly check on suspect information or to make ballpark estimates. Many of these are based on work and resource metrics:

(1) Project Utilization. Individual utilization is usually the prime metric, but aggregation to project utilization is also useful. Project utilization % is defined as project work-hrs/available work-hrs. If this is less than 100%, the PM could increase utilization if the source of the lost utilization can be identified and redirected. If it is more than 100%, overtime is being worked and if sustained may be a problem.

(2) Deliverable Utilization. Deliverable work effort by time period is also worth tracking. If measurements from last month indicate actuals were less than the estimate for the period, then this might mean trouble and require investigation. Was the work over-estimated or resource under-supplied?

(3) Burn Rate. Another important time-related metric is *burn rate*. If the project burn rate is 400 work-hrs/mth, how long does it take to deliver a 10,000 work-hr project at 400 work-hrs/mth? The answer is 25 months. Is this consistent with the committed schedule? The PM keeps on top of the project not only by detailed planning and tracking but by learning to reality check commitments using ROTs.

Resourcing a project adequately is obviously a success criterion, and the responsibility seems to fall mainly on the shoulders of the PM. But all too often, managers of staff over which the PM has no direct control fail to take their own resource obligations seriously and there is no shared data for the parties to review. An improved collaborative approach that entrusts and empowers the PM to maintain comprehensive owner/provider resource plans can eliminate unreliable resource assumptions and should result in better project outcomes.

Specific Resource Guidance

Owner/Provider Guidance

(1) Utilization Categories. Part of the price paid for reporting work metrics is the need to implement a time reporting system and recording by category (project, activity, overhead, etc.). This, I acknowledge, is a controversial requirement. Nobody gets excited about completing a timesheet. To avoid unhelpful discontent, be open about the purpose and importance of the system, and endeavor to keep reporting requirements as simple as possible.

(2) Non-Standard Resources. Some rules should be anticipated to keep utilization measurements meaningful:

- Part-time employees: Percentage utilization is calculated based on available hours, but available hours are reduced to match their part-time contract.
- Contractors: By definition, time and material subcontractors hired for project work are only compensated for project work and thus their percentage utilization is 100%.

(3) Estimating Skills. Unlike the provider, owner resources may be inexperienced in estimating activities. Their work in an operational environment does not typically involve thinking about work-hrs needed to fulfil a scope of work. When asking staff and stakeholders to do such estimating for the project resource plan, managers should be prepared to deal with objections and provide some coaching. Estimating skills can be taught.

Client/Vendor Guidance

(1) Utilization Equals Business. Every vendor knows utilization is a critical metric, if only because of this rule of thumb.

Revenue = Average project utilization × Average rate × No. of practitioners

Time reporting is a necessity for billing time and material contracts. Thus, defining, building, and operating an efficient time reporting system is an absolute priority.

Notes

1 Hornby, Robin. 2017. *Commercial Project Management: A Guide to Selling and Delivering Professional Services*, Routledge.
2 Kerzner, Harold. 2009. *Project Management: A Systems Approach to Planning, Scheduling, and Controlling*, Tenth Edition, John Wiley & Sons Inc.

5 Independent Project Practices

Creating a Delivery Organization, as I mentioned at the outset, is a worthwhile objective for any enterprise which runs more than a handful of simple projects a year. This guide presumes that the basic practices needed to run projects already exist within such an organization. These practices are independent of collaboration between provider and owner but are a foundation for project proficiency. In this, category would be topics such as hiring technical staff, performance management, project management and sponsorship, team building, HR management, business planning for projects, portfolio management, specialized methodologies, project review and audit, and possibly more. Most are large subjects dealt with in the references and are technically beyond the scope of this guide.

There are, however, two important fundamental practices deserving more explanation, so the nascent Delivery Organization can double-check to confirm they are in place. They are the roles and responsibilities of the project sponsor, and the building of project teams.

The Sponsor

The sponsor comes from the owner and is the most important project stakeholder. Larger complex corporate projects require sponsorship from the executive level. More modest projects are sponsored by intermediate management. The sponsor may be the head of the department or business unit to benefit most from the project, usually chairs the steering committee, acts as the senior decision-making authority, and provides (or manages) the funding. In the context of the Delivery Organization, the sponsor is also a key participant in collaborating with the project manager.

During project materialization, it should be self-evident who is designated as sponsor. This person, or an agreed delegate, is likely confirmed by the company's capital planning committee. An early task is to take charge of the DO1 Project Charter, though it is often authored by the provider.

DOI: 10.4324/9781003370031-6

On occasion, while working on the project charter, the PM may discover no sponsor exists, or there is mystery and ambiguity about who it is. In a client/vendor situation, this can probably be tolerated so long as there is a client PM who can assume the essential sponsor responsibilities. In an in-house situation, the provider PM must escalate to provider management who should attempt to resolve the matter based on precedent, politics, and common sense.

The project manager makes every effort to establish a sound business relationship with the sponsor. An interesting question is the exact nature of this relationship. The sponsor is not the PM's boss, as is sometimes thought. The PM's boss is the person in the provider's department who did the hiring. The sponsor is the 'boss' of the project's business profile, and the PM is immediately accountable to the sponsor within that context. But within this scope, the PM retains considerable autonomy as to ways and means of executing the project to achieve the sponsor's business objectives. It is the provider who holds the PM to account for project execution, either through the office of a delivery manager, practice manager, or resource manager. The subtlety of these relationships is often implied using dashed lines on organization charts.

In the section on RAA, Tables 4.1 and 4.2 listed the responsibilities and authorities of a PM. Though it is unlikely a PM will hold all of these on any project, they do provide a checklist, recognizable by most providers. Unfortunately, there is little in the literature to provide an equivalent list for the sponsor. I suggest later a set of informal role descriptions a good sponsor can adopt (or perhaps I have wished sponsors would adopt!).

Executive Role

I have encountered a surprising number of reluctant sponsors, so the first valuable characteristic is to be *willing*. Developing a genuine appreciation for the necessity of the role may help generate enthusiasm. Furthermore, there are real accountabilities as a result of the project proceeding, and reluctance will not help evade them.

The sponsor must understand the essential rationale for the project and fulfil a key role in describing the business benefits, managing their development, and eventually harvesting them. The sponsor must be committed and act as a champion and booster for the project with fellow executives. An important oversight role is to establish a project steering committee comprising key senior stakeholders and schedule monthly (possibly quarterly) meetings.

The sponsor welcomes and approves the project charter as a living foundation for the project and accepts ownership even though others may help create it. It must express clearly the demands made upon the PM and the delegations provided. The sponsor requires the charter to be updated to reflect any changes in roles, objectives, budget, and material risk. During execution, the charter outlines the conditions constituting a go/no-go decision at phase end. At the end of the completion stage, it is the sponsor who determines if the project is complete. Although the opinion of subordinates may be relied upon, it is the sponsor who declares the project over.

Communication with the PM is as precise as possible. An understanding of the project's triple constraint is important, and the sponsor provides meaningful guidance when trade-offs are needed. Discussion on changes is inevitable and the sponsor collaborates with the PM to understand why the change is necessary and who pays for it.

The sponsor must also adopt an executive perspective on project risk. Risk management is a concern of the PM, so the sponsor relies on periodic assessments from the PM. But there are some areas of risk the sponsor can know more about or should. It is a responsibility of the sponsor to understand if the project has exposure to any of the 'mega-risks' in the following list and confidentially discuss them with the PM as appropriate:

Project Mega-risks

- Insufficient funds to continue without impact
- Demands to advance deadline
- Marketplace changes cast doubt on project rationale/benefits
- Project is unjustified, audit pending
- Scope of project is misunderstood, unable to defend
- Government policy changes could eliminate the requirement
- Political opposition in the owner organization
- Pending resignation of sponsor, corporate takeover or amalgamation, or departmental reorganization
- Failure of prime contractor (e.g., bankruptcy, legal proceedings, or negative PR)
- Project obsolescence caused by a rapid change in technology
- Project management incompetence
- Acts of God

There are mitigations in many cases.

Project Manager Support Role

The sponsor may be the 'business boss' of the PM, but the most effective view of the relationship is as a team – both are nurturing the project with their complementary responsibilities, skills, and knowledge. The sponsor shows respect for the PM's mandate and unless proven otherwise, operates the relationship based on mutual trust. Acting as a guide to the PM in relevant areas – internal politics, corporate history, prejudices held by important stakeholders – can also be very helpful.

The sponsor's decision-making role is a key project success factor, and a positive and engaged relationship with the PM increases the reliability of decisions made within the mandate of either party. Often, subordinates are tempted to tell their superiors 'what they want to hear'. A sponsor can counteract this by demanding an honest opinion and not creating pressure to provide false status. By the same token, the PM prefers not to be kept guessing about what is important and what should take priority. It also helps if the sponsor reads, and questions, the PM's project status reports.

Accessibility, with reasonable notice, gives the PM confidence though this privilege should not be abused. An excellent idea is to schedule a series of regular review meetings with the PM; 30 minutes is enough, with the understanding a meeting may be canceled or rescheduled if other duties intervene.

Team Support Role

Many team members and stakeholders know (at least from a distance) and respect the sponsor, whereas the PM may not radiate quite the same aura, especially if from a vendor. This allows the sponsor to play a useful, motivational, and team-building role.

I recall many successful projects when occasional pitches from the sponsor were enjoyed by the entire team. At the kickoff meeting, naturally, but also throughout the project after a specific milestone or achievement, the team always welcomed encouragement, recognition, and a more personal account of what the project meant to the sponsor and the company. And, depending on the personality of the sponsor, it's always fun to hear some senior scuttlebutt relating to the project or showing the project or senior team members in a good light. It's also a nice touch for the sponsor to meet new senior team members when they join, get to know them personally, and deliver a few standard messages informally. This supplements the exhortations the team hears from the PM.

If there is trust between the sponsor and PM, both will be attentive to constructive comments on team performance. The project manager certainly wants to hear about any team issues that have reached the ears of the sponsor, and the sponsor is hopefully open to frank feedback from the PM on how things could be improved in the owner's management chain.

Client/Vendor Guidance

(1) Sponsor Access. Although the vendor provider is often placed in a parallel team structure, sometimes the reporting is direct to a client PM who reports to the sponsor. In this case, the vendor PM might find access to the sponsor is curtailed and the relationship more distant, the sponsor preferring to deal solely with the owner's PM. I used to worry about this arrangement, but so long as the owner's PM is delegated to deal with the issues and decisions as required, then it needn't be a detriment.

(2) Steering Committee Membership. One of the executive duties of the sponsor is to establish a project steering committee, which the sponsor usually chairs. An issue I have often faced is who represents the vendor, or whether the vendor is represented at all. In the case of a client PM with the vendor as a direct subordinate, I have been told the project is adequately represented by the more senior PM, and I can stay at home! At the other extreme, with a very welcoming client and a large project, I have attended steering committee meetings as the PM in the company of the salesman and the delivery manager. This can be a complicated matter and the best solution is very situational. The only certain recommendation is *someone* with a working knowledge of the project should represent the vendor. If the vendor PM is overshadowed by the owner PM, then it should be the vendor delivery manager.

My observation is steering committees rarely act as spontaneous decision-making bodies but focus on reviewing, recommending, and consensus-building. Regardless of who attends, weighty matters will always be subject to ratification 'back at headquarters'.

The Project Team

The job of the provider is to create and maintain a project team. In fact, most of the provider's work will be done through projects, and in the case of a vendor, all of it. There are several important abilities exercised by the provider and the PM when building project teams. Chief among these tasks are hiring, ensuring team training and compatibility, preparing statements of role, assessing performance, managing team behavior, resolving conflict, coaching, and using these softer people management skills specified in *Human Resource Skills for the Project Manager*.[1] There are two areas I need to explore in some detail; the statement of role because it deserves more widespread use, and performance management because PMs are often unsure of their approach to this responsibility, which can cause work and relationships to suffer.

Statement of Role

Every job position on a project team needs a defined and written Statement of Role (SOR). These are prepared once and reviewed and updated periodically. In software development, a generic SOR might be generated for the roles of developer, analyst, technical specialist, consultant, project manager, and others. Perhaps each has two or three seniority levels. Specific projects can then use these as templates to be customized to fit their staffing needs.

Building a comprehensive SOR can call on a checklist of skills and attributes including experience and achievements, professional or peer standing, competencies, occupational knowledge, technical skills, personal skills (including managerial and professional), behavioral traits, and personality. Technical skills and knowledge map directly to the work to be performed, and experience requirements are usually related to the seniority, supervisory responsibilities, and complexity inherent in the role.

Personality and behavior are complex attributes to assess but should not be ignored. What is the best way to deal with personality without a degree in psychology? One useful approach is to simplify the matter into organizational and cultural 'fit' or chemistry. The SOR should then identify the critical groups and individuals with whom positive chemistry is required.

Behavioral traits are the observable manifestations of personality and can be neutral, positive, or negative in relation to the role. One role might suit a natural skeptic, another someone who is painstaking. Some roles may not suit someone who interrupts or is impatient and hurried. These behavioral characteristics can be analyzed and assessed. One solution to the assessment problem is to adopt a behavioral model based on the Myers–Briggs type indicators. There are many such commercial models available; a good example is described in *Personal Styles & Effective Performance*,[2] and a simple test can give read-outs on an individual's business orientation based on behavioral traits. These models work with the type indicators to place subjects into groups useful for business purposes. For example:

Behavioral Traits

- A strategic thinker with a creative trait
- An entrepreneurial outlook with a desire to build
- An organizer with an interest in making things work better
- A technical orientation interested in sustaining operations

How much does the role demand of each of these behavioral traits? The SOR might at least provide a brief overview of the most suitable orientation for the role. Remember, tests are useful to identify the *dominant* traits, because everyone exhibits these traits to some degree. Also, when staffing or hiring a resource who demonstrates a compatible orientation for the role, be aware these descriptors do not signify the presence of skill or achievements; they are only measures of behavior and represent the individual's preferences.

Whether building a team in-house, hiring, or selecting a contractor, an SOR is really a prerequisite and can be used as a base for interviewing, candidate selection, and as we shall see in the next section, performance evaluation.

Performance Management

As previously quoted, if you can't measure it, then you can't manage it. But applying this rule to the performance of employees is difficult and contentious. I have never found a manager or an employee who looks forward to the annual appraisal. Perhaps that's why appraisals are often poorly done. Structured or unstructured, rated or qualitative, using a bell curve model or not, 360-degree input, self-evaluation or manager only, formal or informal – I think I have seen all variants and enjoyed none of them! Part of the problem lies in ambiguity and co-dependency often found in responsibilities for regular operations work. The project environment, however, is designed for clarity of responsibility and does provide an opportunity to reliably assess the performance of individuals. If certain guidelines are followed, assessments can be helpful in strengthening both individual and team performance.

Regardless of company policy, the PM is obliged by the role to hold a team member accountable for the performance of their work. If the company does operate a formal performance management scheme, then those policies govern the PM's official responsibilities. Most likely annual appraisals will be done, and compensation may be linked. The project manager will probably be requested to provide input regarding employees who worked on projects during the year. Every employee should be aware of this. Also, a good performance system differentiates between achievements and skill levels. The former acts primarily as a contributor to promotion prospects, and the latter might indicate training needs. If performance consistently fails to meet requirements of the SOR, then the PM is justified in seeking a replacement. However, if the company operates a formal Performance Improvement Program (PIP), the PM may be party to this and should be familiar with prevailing government labor law. Usually, the program is an attempt at recovery, in which case the employee is told clearly and in writing the improvements expected and the minimum results required over a defined period, usually 3 months. If these are not achieved, then the employee may be terminated.

I have always considered project managers to be in a fortunate position when it comes to the perplexing business of evaluating employee performance. Compared to other pursuits, a project abounds in objectives, milestones, budgets, deadlines, and opportunities to demonstrate initiative, reliability, creativity, and intelligence. All this is grist to the mill of performance evaluation. The framework for the evaluation can be based on the SOR for the project position and on the performance chains specified for the project. This can be fitted to the format required by the corporate system and forwarded to the employee's boss (assuming it's someone other than the PM). Should this be shared with the employee? Yes, though not in a lump but incrementally through the life of the project as a natural project activity. This is part of a feedback system the PM owes to the team member during their task completions, and they should be alerted to expect it as part of the management process. Using judgment, the PM may also choose to initiate informal coaching or recommend specific training.

The project manager also makes it part of the job to observe team members in group sessions with their peers or in formal sessions with the owner. This includes meetings to review issues or project progress. The formal PM's role at these gatherings is to respond to resource-related issues and take away any requested action plans. But these are also valuable opportunities to observe team members in a business setting and note any negative behaviors to be addressed later by feedback and coaching. During breaks, a gentle, informal "how are we doing?" question may also be asked of the owner.

Coaching is a term borrowed from sports and has found application elsewhere, including projects (and life). It addresses one simple goal – performance improvement. This may be the ambition of either the PM or the team member, though hopefully both. Good coaching of individuals is well structured, conveniently timed, and private. Coaching can be provided by anyone who possesses the required knowledge or experience, and any senior member of a project team should be prepared to assist junior members in this manner. In many cases, PMs are ideally placed to provide coaching. I believe it is such an important aspect of their job; it should be written into their SOR.

Coaching works well when applied to immediate problems related to the job at hand. One method is to demonstrate use of a progressive problem-solving method and then provide feedback as a solution is developed. Another is to teach a specific technique and then review its application. Though feedback is given privately, public demonstrations may be useful in workshops or in actual real-life project situations. The project manager may not have the technical skills of the team member but can contribute knowledge of methods and techniques seen in previous projects.

Therefore, I believe the PM is a natural coach and should be recognized more widely for this role.

Coaching and mentoring are often treated as synonymous, though there is a distinction. The employee chooses a mentor as an inspiration; it is not someone assigned the task of improving performance. Of course, a mentor may occasionally choose to act as coach. The mentor is senior, established, professionally respected, demonstrates traits the employee admires, acts as a role model, and is in a position to help. A senior project manager can indeed make a good mentor. I can think of four mentors in my career; two were my direct boss at the time, one was my project director on a large project, and one was a very senior consultant I worked with on a challenging assignment.

Notes

1 Verma, Vijay K. 1995. *Human Resource Skills for the Project Manager*, Project Management Institute, Inc.
2 Merrill, David W. and Reid, Roger H. 1981. *Personal Styles & Effective Performance*, Chilton Book Company.

6 Implementation Steps

In this penultimate chapter, I lay out a roadmap of implementation steps to create the Delivery Organization. This invites the risk of making the venture sound onerous and excessively akin to major undertakings the reader might have experienced, such as ISO9000 or development methodology implementation. This is not so. In a typical organization, it is more analogous to reshaping how they see the project world and collecting elements already found in hidden pockets, refurbishing them, and making them visible and readily available in the improved environment – an environment freshly streamlined for collaborative project achievement.

Collaboration Summary

To set the scene for implementation, the summary in Figure 6.1 takes all the components I've defined as contributing to a collaborative, business-oriented project environment, and maps them on two axes.

On the horizontal scale from left to right is an assessment of the ease of implementation. On the vertical axis, the height of the bar is a representation of the value contributed to owner and provider collaboration. As you might expect, I endorse the implementation of each element and practice, but implementation of each element and practice is entirely optional. The organization can proceed based on any degree of take-up with no penalty, after considering the difficulty and value of each implementation group:

Implementation Groups

(1) Core DO Elements. These are the 10 business lifecycle collaboration elements (processes, reviews, documents, techniques) I consider indispensable ranging from the project charter to project sign-off. They are an inherent part of any common project management method, and the

DOI: 10.4324/9781003370031-7

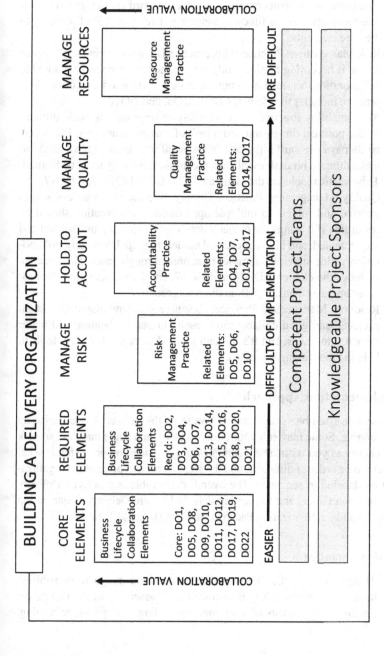

Figure 6.1 Building a Delivery Organization

only requirement is to adapt them to a proper collaborative process. This is the benchmark for ease of implementation.

(2) Required DO Elements. These are the remaining 12 business lifecycle collaboration elements ranging from the standard checklists to innovative elements such as lifecycle mapping. They are second in value to the core elements.

(3) Risk Management Practice. This practice is rated next in ease because its use is becoming familiar and many of the tools are easily adapted to collaboration. Value is high but dependent upon good execution. This practice includes the elements DO5, DO6, and DO10.

(4) Accountability Practice. Accountability management is made difficult by the political dimension and a lack of classic techniques. But it certainly pays a reward if the collaborative effort is made. I have aimed to make things a bit easier with new techniques, but they must be learned. This practice includes the elements DO4, DO7, DO14, and DO17.

(5) Quality Management Practice. Quality is difficult because it's specialized and subject to multiple approaches. Collaboration should be rewarding if it brings the owner's needs closer to being understood and implemented, and I have presented models to help. Ultimately, collaboration yields incremental rather than breakthrough gains. This practice includes the elements DO14 and DO17, and I am presuming the provider operates a basic QMS in the background.

(6) Resource Management Practice. Resource problems haunt almost all projects, and good collaboration results in better planning and better response to issues. But it's a tough job and there are few easy tools to help the management process.

Implementation Approach

This section assembles some ideas on how to get the Delivery Organization up and running. Some may suit your circumstances, and some may not, so pick and choose as you wish. The techniques and practices are presented in what I deem to be order of difficulty, and the steps needed to prepare the organization are labeled in sequence. The overall deliverable is a tailored Delivery Organization Guide, and supporting deliverables are Delivery Organization Training and Familiarization Package, and PM Business Training.

Getting Organized

STEP1 Appoint a DOC. The organization needs to assign responsibility. The immediate responsibility is overseeing the assembly of the DO guide. The ongoing role consists of selecting, responding to requests, refreshing, and maybe expanding the collection. After the start-up it should only require a few hours per week. The candidate entities for this responsibility were discussed in the section *Organizational Innovations*.

STEP2 Assess Current Situation. The concept of the DO relies on an existing implementation of project management and project sponsorship. Taking nothing for granted, I suggest the DOC takes stock of where the organization currently stands. Is the position of project manager officially recognized? Are basic PM tools, techniques, and processes understood and used? Are at least most of the core elements in place, with or without collaboration? Are project sponsors officially recognized? Are there written documents explaining their role and responsibilities? In the absence of such a document, is there a consistency of response when asking owner-managers those questions?

If some of these assessment questions are answered negatively or are hard to answer, time and effort might be best spent developing basic competencies before adding the formalization of the DO.

STEP3 Adopt the Frameworks. These have been extensively discussed, and I am hoping the reader shares my opinion that establishing a regime of working methods is easier if there is a conceptual reference showing how the details are connected. These are frameworks that assist DO implementation and require a place in the DO guide:

Frameworks to Support the DO

(1) Business Lifecycle. Very important to adopt, primarily because it steers attention to business matters, unifies delivery among different providers, and creates a relatable reference language for management. All the DO elements are mapped to the business lifecycle. The collaborative approach to risk is specifically predicated on it.

(2) Four Functions of Project Management. Viewing the work of the PM in terms of planning, organizing, controlling, and leading (POCL) facilitates the debate between multiple PMs when striving to delineate their shared responsibilities. It's not mandatory, just very helpful.

(3) Project Lifecycle. This comes from the provider and must be there, other than for the simplest of projects. The DO benefit is to use it as a tool of integration.

(4) Owner/Provider Balance. The use of this model provides an analogy to help stakeholders understand the need for, and the real nature of deliverable and system acceptance.

STEP4 Determine How to Build the DO Guide. Throughout the following implementation notes, there are comments on the need for forms, templates, briefing notes, and instructions to include in the guide. The technology must be designated and used consistently in constructing these elements. A structure for the content needs to be designed. The guide content expected from most of the following steps must be specified.

Implement DO Elements

STEP5 Choose a Development Approach. There are 22 elements. Some require a form to be designed, a document template to be created, checklist to be made, and a technique or process to be written up. The work can be split into two stages, first the 10 core elements, and then the remaining 12. Each element is effectively standalone (a few exceptions) so selection and sequence are independent. I can't think of any reason to omit any of the 10 core elements (except perhaps initially the risk elements because they require some familiarity with risk techniques). For the remaining 12, some selections may be omitted for a first release until more experience is gained. These might include the more labor-intensive reports: DO15 Phase End, DO16 Dashboard, DO18 Transition, and DO20 Satisfaction Survey. DO21 Performance Evaluation is problematic and depends upon current policies, processes, and organizational culture.

STEP6 Develop Each Element. Among the 10 core elements, there will already be an existing stock of templates, forms, and associated instructions. These should be appropriated and declared as collaborative elements and new usage instructions written to explain the role to be adopted by owner and provider. For the 12 required elements, the approach can be the same, starting with the less onerous – DO2, DO3, DO4, DO7, DO13, and DO14. The summary Table 3.1 is a good context for assessing this work.

Note the implementation steps for elements taken from the professional practices are repeated in the following practice implementation sections where more guidance will be found.

Implement Risk Practice

STEP7 Determine Enhancements to Existing Practice. It is likely the provider already operates some form of risk analysis and management, so the first step is to determine the upgrades required. The risk practice includes the core elements DO5, DO6, and DO10, so if these are to be implemented then so should the risk event, risk planning, and risk execution models.

STEP8 How to Assess Lifecycle Risk. The risk lifecycle model offers a global view of risk meshed with the business lifecycle. It is a great framework to facilitate collaborative risk management. A corporate risk guide can be developed to assist with the risk questions to be asked at each stage.

It should be prepared by someone with experience in project risk theory and practice, to be endorsed by the DOC for inclusion in the guide. Some training for stakeholders might also be useful, such as the fishbone diagram, cause-and-effect model, and other tools.

STEP9 How to Analyze Risk Events. This risk analysis is based on the risk event model. The cause-and-effect event model is easy to explain and underpins classic risk analysis. The output is the DO5 Risk Register, one of the core elements, initiated during project planning and periodically updated during execution. An excellent collaborative process is to develop the risk register at a series of brainstorming workshops, with the objective of identifying risks, classifying them in terms of impact, and then developing mitigations starting with the high-impact risks. A facilitator with sound risk management experience is recommended.

STEP10 Build a Risk Factor Checklist (Planning Stage). The risk factor checklist is based on the risk planning model and supports the element DO6. The planning model is much easier to apply than the risk event model, but it does need to be designed and coded, either simply on Excel or as a web page solution. Risk experience is needed in the design, which lists and characterizes a dozen or so risk factors in the environment, but then can be used by individuals with less experience. The assessment of severity of factors can be facilitated by a PM or lead analyst. To illustrate the method, Table 6.1 lists four questions for risk factors associated with the facet 'Team'. Together with questions for risk factors from the other facets, they make up a risk factor checklist.

STEP11 Build a Risk Alert Checklist (Execution Stage). The risk alert checklist is based on the risk execution model and supports the core element D10. The execution model is like the planning model. A standard list of risk alerts (or health checks) is developed and then assessed in a joint meeting. The output is the DO10 Risk Alert Checklist which provides an assessment of each performance chain. Table 6.2 shows monthly severity ratings (red,

Table 6.1

Risk Factor Questions to Assess a Facet

FACET TEAM	RISK FACTOR QUESTION	MAX RISK RESPONSE	MAX RISK POINTS
Q1	Are the skills available in-house?	No	4
Q2	Will the team be co-located?	No	4
Q3	Are there cultural dissimilarities?	Yes	3
Q4	Has the team worked together before?	No	4
TOTAL			15

Table 6.2

Scheme for a Risk Alert Checklist

Project:
Client:
Period covered by report:
Report completed by:

PERFORMANCE CHAIN CHECKLIST		Jan	Feb	Mar	Apr	May	Jun
PART 1 DELIVERY		Enter R/Y/G as per guidance in parentheses					
1 Milestones	Delayed by more than 5 days in the last period? (no, anticipated, yes)						
2 External Dependencies	Being rescheduled? (no, anticipated, yes)						
3 Technical Problems	Are chronic technical problems being encountered? (no, resolutions identified, yes)						
4 Contract	Is the contract being adhered to? (yes, difficulties, no)						
5 . . .							

---

yellow, green) based on the response chosen for alerts in the 'Delivery' performance chain.

STEP12 Add Custom Risk Alert Extensions. The standard performance chains can be expanded to meet the customized requirements of specific owner-focused objectives. A checklist of possible objectives to be added to the DO10 Alert Checklist is shown in Table 4.3.

STEP13 Tune Risk Tools. After a period of use, say 3 to 6 months, the tools should be reviewed. Some factors and alerts may be removed, and perhaps others added. The ratings may be recalibrated based on experience.

Implement Accountability Practice

Accountability tools may be unfamiliar and incorrectly perceived as 'micro-management', and they all require some degree of proceduralization and documentation. The DOC may prefer implementation be phased as experience and DO maturity is gained. However, a benefit of moving forward more quickly is that they are the most tangible elements in this practice and their use is easy to review and audit.

STEP14 Create Stakeholder Awareness. Building accountability in an organization (or project) is a management process supported by a cultural understanding. Implementation requires senior management engagement and a heightened awareness by all stakeholders. The guide should include a briefing on RAA theory, using the section *Responsibility, Accountability, and Authority (RAA)* to build this awareness.

STEP15 Selection of Team Structure. Based on the section *Project Structure and Accountability*, the DOC reviews options with the owner and provider to assess which are viable for the company, and under which circumstances these options are to be preferred. The guide should include a briefing on team structure selection to be referenced by the sponsor following the materialization stage. This then supports the team structure decision to be made for new projects.

STEP16 Implement Lifecycle Mapping. This is the first of three accountability tools defined in the section *Project Structure and Accountability* whose main purpose is to support collaborative assignment of responsibilities in core element DO4. This technique is an adaptation of the table used to integrate team and project management deliverables for each phase. In larger projects with PMs leading different teams, or an owner PM and a provider PM, this table is used to define project management deliverables and activities in their entirety. The example in Table 6.3, showing just two phases of a project, should help the reader understand the outcome of the process, though the phase column will depend on the project lifecycle being used, and the actual PM activities and deliverables will depend upon the project management standards and methods. For each listed activity and deliverable, the PMs collaboratively determine the ownership of the item, and the degree of collaboration required.

The map table is largely customized by the PMs when the project starts. If not already available from the provider, a checklist of PM deliverables and activities could be prepared for the DO guide to assist during the mapping session.

STEP17 Implement Responsibility Assignment Matrix (RAM). This is the second of three accountability tools defined in the section *Project Structure and Accountability* whose main purpose is to support the collaborative assignment of responsibilities in element DO7. This is primarily a tool for collaboration between owner/provider PMs and stakeholders. The purpose is to agree and unambiguously document responsibilities for important deliverables. The example in Table 6.4 is the best way of understanding the output documentation. This postulates six activities required to create a Specifications Report. Each activity is tagged with a PARIS code for each involved stakeholder. PARIS coding means the following:

Table 6.3

Project Lifecycle Mapping of PM Deliverables

PHASE OF LIFECYCLE	ACTIVITIES FOR PM COLLABORATION				DELIVERABLES FOR PM COLLABORATION
	PLAN	ORGANIZE	CONTROL	LEAD	
1 REQUIREMENTS	Develop mandate Plan the activities Establish priorities	Define responsibilities and procedures	Evaluate activity completion Provide feedback	Verify CBA Set objectives Align stakeholders	Project charter Project procedures manual RAM Requirements sign-off
2 GENERAL DESIGN	Plan the activities Set design direction	Induct team members Establish communication	Approve designs Trace to requirements	Build team Fit to business	Project plan Communications plan Design sign-off Project status report
3 …					

Table 6.4

Using the RAM Technique for a Project Deliverable based on Activities

SPECIFICATIONS REPORT (ACTIVITIES)	STAKEHOLDERS						
	VENDOR PM	TEAM LEADER	TEAM	CLIENT TECHN REP	OPERATIONS MANAGER	SYSTEM USERS	SPONSOR
Prepare plan	A,P	P,R		I	I	I	S
Gather requirements	S	A,P	P	I	I	I	I
Validate requirements with contract	S,A,P	P	P	R	R		S
Ensure requirements are technically feasible	S,A,P	P					S
Prepare conceptual designs	S	A,P	P	I,R	I,R		S
Prepare Specifications Report	S	A,P	P	R	R	R	S

Definition of PARIS Coding

Participate: Means to 'do' and carry responsibility for activity(s) that contribute to the result.

Accountable: Means to be assigned overall responsibility for the result, to have the necessary authority, and may be judged on the success of the endeavor. Organization theory suggests there only be one Accountable person per line item.

Review: Means to assess deliverables, performance, or results, and may have specialist knowledge, responsibilities, or experience. Often, the Sign-off person will look to Reviewers for validation of approval.

Input: Means to provide data, information, techniques, and opinion, usually on request.

Sign-off: Means to formally end the phase of work designed to get the result. There may be more than one Sign-off individual each approving from a different perspective.

Implementation work for RAM includes instructions in the guide for completing an RAM table and preparing template tables using deliverables from the provider's methodology. Level of detail should also be considered – should the RAM specify PARIS codes for deliverables, or for detailed activities as shown in the example in Table 6.4? This itemizes activities to create a Specifications Report deliverable.

STEP18 Implement Deliverable Acceptance. This is the third of three accountability tools defined in the section *Project Structure and Accountability* whose main purpose is to support collaborative assignment of responsibilities. This procedure is based on the duality quality model, where the obligations of the supplier are recognized and balanced by the obligations of the acceptor. Implementation requires a procedure to be written and a template form for signature by the sign-off authorities. DO14 Deliverable Acceptance is the outcome of this process, and the section *Owner/Provider Balance* includes a complete template process for the entire acceptance procedure and is not repeated here. DO14 is classified within both the accountability and quality practice (see STEP25 Design the Acceptance Process).

Implement a Basic QMS

This implementation is intended for a provider who needs to address the quality issue from square one. It provides a starting point for a provider beginning with quality, taken from the more detailed explanations in the section *Quality Management*. Providers with quality experience and an existing QMS implementation can integrate the collaborative quality models they consider helpful into their existing implementation.

STEP19 Prepare a Quality Policy Statement. This is prepared, endorsed, and distributed by the provider's executive. It goes beyond a simple statement of commitment and explains in a few paragraphs what the commitment entails, using the quality triangle as a template. The following is a brief illustrative example, not a specific recommendation:

"Project managers are to prepare a quality plan for every project, and to ensure execution using a checklist. All employees should be trained for their roles with a target budget of 10 days per year. All projects are to be planned in MS Project and must integrate with personal calendars used by team members".

Every project person should see the impact upon themselves in the policy.

STEP20 Build a Quality Support Environment. Keeping overhead costs low is an initial objective, but quality cannot be mandated without committing some level of support. A minimum starting point would be developing templates for the project quality plan and the quality execution checklists. Every role description (SOR) is reviewed to ensure the employee's specific quality responsibilities are described. Templates using MS Project are developed for different classes of project undertaken by the provider. A two-hour workshop to explain the QMS and the rationale for each element is developed and presented to all project employees and all new employees in the future.

STEP21 How to Prepare Project Quality Plans. The quality plan is a flexible document, but a page or so within the overall project plan is suggested for the basic QMS. A checklist format can also be considered. The purpose is to describe how the project will achieve the agreed quality objectives, explaining the use of standards, techniques, responsibilities, methods, and metrics. This includes commitment to the provider's QC/QA processes.

STEP22 How to Execute the Quality Plan. The project executes under the mandate of the project plan, delivering the quality requirements specified in the quality plan. The project manager uses checklists for the establishment of objectives, assignment of activities, and the completion of deliverables. The PM maintains ongoing observation of all elements in the quality plan and provides relevant feedback to team members offering praise or correction.

Implement Collaborative Quality Models

The models are fully described in the section *Four Quality Models* and used to design a collaborative process. The point model is especially useful in revealing the owner's real quality needs, but it requires knowledge of the project technology, user requirements, and a willingness to learn the technique. The quadrant model demands engagement from the collaborating participants, but a confident and patient approach yields better compromises and therefore a better project.

STEP23 How to Establish Project Objectives. This is an important collaborative procedure and requires description in the guide to be endorsed by the DOC. The owner, supported by the provider, is obliged to articulate a clear description of the business objectives to be achieved by the project. The next step is to derive exactly what the project must deliver to meet those objectives. This is not always obvious and may require several discussions between owner and provider. The result is an important step in overall project definition, establishing project objectives and deliverables. From this information, the quality requirements can be extracted, and the point model used to elaborate from the owner's expression of system quality to specific quality objectives, then to implementable quality factors.

STEP24 How to Establish Quality Factors. The questions from the point model in the section *Four Quality Models* are as follows: What are your quality goals for the product? How will you know if your quality goals are met? What product feature would contribute to each of these objectives? The guide can list a selection, or checklist, of supporting detail questions to help cover the domain of quality possibilities (e.g., system life, durability, error tolerance, conformance to commercial or technical standards, ease of usage, ease of maintenance, adaptability, expandability, and so forth). Collaborative work requires an owner familiar with the quality requirements, and a provider with good technical knowledge who can assess cost and feasibility. I recommend each identified factor be tagged with a priority such as 'need, want, nice-to-have' for reference if subsequent trade-off negotiations are required.

STEP25 Design the Acceptance Process. This is derived from the second of the quality models defined in *Four Quality Models*. The procedure is based on the duality quality model, where the obligations of the supplier are recognized and balanced by the obligations of the acceptor. Implementation requires a procedure to be written and a template form for signature by the sign-off authorities. DO14 Deliverable Acceptance is the outcome of this process, and the section *Owner/Provider Balance* includes a very complete template process for the entire acceptance procedure and is not repeated here. DO14 is classified within both the accountability (see STEP18 Implement Deliverable Acceptance) and the quality practice.

STEP26 How to Assign Activities. This is derived from the third of the quality models defined in *Four Quality Models* and activity assignment is envisaged as a collaboration between PM and team member. When the team member is assigned, the three fundamentals of the triangle quality model (People, Process, and Technology) are discussed and expectations for the execution of the activity are settled. The instructions could include a

Table 6.5

Trade-off Considerations

PRODUCT FUNCTIONALITY	PROJECT COST
1. Delivery of *all* functions	1. Fixed limits
2. 'Need, want, nice to have'	2. Quarterly/annual budget limits
3. Ease of use	3. External costs vs. internal costs
4. Consistency of interfaces	4. Resource constraints
5. Performance characteristics	5. Resource replacement
6. Data integration	6. Overtime
	7. Overhead/expenses
	8. Re-use
PRODUCT QUALITY OBJECTIVES/FACTORS	PROJECT SCHEDULE
1. System longevity	1. Benefits dependency on date
2. MTBF (or residual defects)	2. Schedule dependency or fit with client activity
3. Maintainability	3. External drivers (e.g., government)
4. Training ease	4. Delivery date commitment
5. Documentation	5. Product release strategy
6. Testability	
7. System resilience	
8. Technology platform	
9. Obsolescence	
10. Grade requirements	

provider checklist of options or mandatories to consider for each part of the triangle. Note the PM explicitly advises the team member when the activity must begin.

STEP27 Design the Trade-off Process. This is derived from the fourth of the quality models defined in *Four Quality Models*. If schedule and budget allocations are exceeded, trade-offs must be designed to reduce work. The quadrant model provides a collaborative framework for negotiation.

Instructions on how to use this model are required, including a checklist of discussion points for each quadrant, as illustrated in Table 6.5. This should lead to a balanced trade-off. Note the downgrading of quality factors, or removal of the less critical functionalities, will likely have an impact on forecast maintenance budgets.

Implement Resource Practice

There is one very large inconsistency between vendor and client resource management which contributes to the difficulty of building common ground, always required for successful collaboration. This, of course, is the practice of time reporting. For a vendor, it represents the lifeblood of the business – revenue equals hours worked times rate. For the client, it seems totally unnecessary. The DO is unlikely to make a considerable effort to implement time reporting for purely speculative gains; thus, it does not belong in an implementation for an embryonic DO. Sophisticated providers, however, will recognize that their estimating skills will be reinforced if actual effort is available to compare with their deliverable estimates.

Most of the useful resource reports and applications described in the section *Resource Management* require time reporting as a prerequisite, so my suggestion is limited to the project resource plan shown in Table 6.6, for which time reporting is not required.

STEP28 Design a Resource Plan Template. Resource forecasting is familiar to the provider, uncomplicated (but not easy), and seems to offer the most benefit from collaboration with the owner. The result is a single forecast integrating provider and owner resources. A template can be created using the example of a project resource plan shown in Table 6.6. A more detailed and useful version breaks out all the activities for each resource and the utilization for each. Most project data can be maintained in a project management tool; Microsoft Project is a common example. Each month the report is generated using updated estimate data provided by the PM. The output shows the work-hrs of effort required per month from each resource over the time horizon of the project. (If the report is granular, say a weekly or monthly period, it is more usual to show expected utilization in work-hrs rather than as a percentage.)

This report can be used for long-term planning and as a short-term check on immediate requirements. Naturally, the near-term data are expected to be the most reliable.

STEP29 Design a Joint Forecasting Process. A protocol for collaborative review and response between owner and provider might be as follows:

Table 6.6

Format of Project Resource Plan

PERIOD RESOURCE	JAN	FEB	MAR	APR	MAY	JUN	JUL	AUG	SEPT	OCT
Resource A		100	200	100		100	50			
Resource B				150	150	150	150	150	100	
Resource C	100	150	150	50					150	100
. . .										
TOTAL WORK- HRS **2100**	200	350	400	200	250	200	150	100	150	100

Collaborative Resource Forecasting

(1) Joint Planning. Based on established project objectives, the PM initially puts forward a draft of the resource plan, including all needed owner and provider resources, though the owner resources are the provider's view of requirements, not commitments. But they dovetail with the provider's plan and meet task requirements. Thus, the plan contains resource information for *both* parties.

(2) Negotiation. Project resourcing issues can be identified, and solutions negotiated. This might include the addition of external resources, adjustment of timeframes, or alteration of work.

(3) Update by Provider. Monthly, it is the job of the PM to reassess plans and make any changes required by approved change orders, resource inadequacies, or poorly estimated work. In this collaboration, the PM must be empowered to speak with all stakeholders with responsibilities in the plan to ensure they are still able to keep their commitments. The new project plan is distributed to the parties listed in the communication plan. The resource forecast is sent to the owner.

(4) Joint Review. Monthly, the parties meet to review the new resource forecast and establish commitment to whatever changes have been made. Additional changes authorized at this review might include overtime, adding external resources, adjustment of timeframes, or alteration of work.

Complete DO Implementation

The remaining identified work is to prepare a training kit. I have suggested some other steps to tie up loose ends, but much of the remaining implementation depends on the organization.

STEP30 Develop Training Material. There is little training needed for most stakeholders, but it should not be ignored. Perhaps a better term for the requirement is familiarization. The target audience is all the provider's managers, professional staff, all the owner's management, and those of their staff likely to be engaged in future project work. The session requires about two hours for a full DO implementation.

The material is based on the corporate DO guide with an introduction to explain the main differences between the current organization and the target Delivery Organization. Collaboration is introduced as a way of working, and a distinction can be drawn between cooperating to get a result versus each party working exclusively to further their own interests. Collaboration does not mean you cannot argue for your own viewpoint, but if an impasse is reached the solution may be found by considering the bigger picture. Perhaps most importantly, collaboration means sharing meaningfully in an activity according to one's expected role, skills, and knowledge, and not abrogating into indifference. Introductory examples can be given showing the effect of the new paradigm and the likely benefits.

Each of the 22 elements is presented, featuring its purpose and how it is used. Each of the practices being implemented can be covered in a 15-minute discussion-based segment, bearing in mind when executed the activity will be facilitated by a provider analyst who possesses the necessary specialization.

At the start of a project, a DO familiarization package is circulated to each stakeholder reminding them of expectations and requesting they advise staff in their orbit who will be involved.

STEP31 Miscellaneous. Some further ideas might be useful depending on the culture and experience of the organization. They include establishing a DO oversight committee to support the DO Curator, concentrating more on the facilitation role for each of the practice areas, and preparing a one-page checklist of DO elements and selected practice techniques (a 'cheat sheet'). As good examples of some of the less-familiar documents are collected, they could be retained and shared to help new projects.

Business Skills for Project Managers

Recall that aligning project management with business concerns is a major goal of the DO. The need for knowledge of standard project management processes and their supporting techniques is now widely recognized, but to achieve the goal of the DO, PMs also need business and organizational knowledge. The result of a competency evaluation may signal the need for additional training. Training for the business management of projects is customized to the business model and priorities of the company and includes the core topics shown in Table 6.7.

Table 6.7

Listing of core topics for business training of PMs

TOPICS

Accountabilities practice	Estimate counselling
Business and finance basics	Project status for owners
Quality management practice	Lifecycle mapping
Revenue accounting	Authority delegations
The business lifecycle	Executive dashboard
Risk management practice	Performance evaluation
Contract management	Procurement practice

A certain amount of business delegation is also granted to PMs. As project managers gain business skills and experience, then they can be granted delegation commensurate with the value and criticality of the project. The use of an internal authority table is a succinct way for the DO to document delegations and is easily understood by PMs.

As project management expands to include a business perspective, owners likewise need an appreciation of project principles. Application of certain project management disciplines on the owner side will increase the effectiveness of the DO. Quality management, risk management, and understanding the business implications of project status are three examples.

Client/Vendor Guidance

(1) Vendor Business. In the client/vendor case, the vendor PM is also under pressure to understand and work toward the firm's business objectives, and this includes the obligation for the project to return a profit. This is an important item on the vendor's business training curriculum.

7 The Future of Collaboration

The business lifecycle is the foundation for building a Delivery Organization. The reader will recall the project materialization part of the lifecycle, which was left undeveloped while I explored collaborative ideas for the delivery stages. This chapter returns to the materialization stage to see whether useful collaboration can indeed be achieved, and under what conditions.

The project architecture in Figure 2.1 acknowledged the need for two paths through materialization; one path if development is in-house, and an alternate path if the project is contracted to a vendor. These two worlds are quite different, as the *Client/Vendor* notes have frequently suggested. Table 7.1 presents a summary of the more consequential differences.

Collaboration is self-evidently an easier proposition for the owner and in-house provider, whereas the client/vendor case is considerably more challenging. It is the latter case we wish to explore.

Avoidable Losses in the Classic System

Presuming the client has completed a brief feasibility or preliminary requirements study and the high-level cost/benefit assessment described in the section *Project Materialization Stage*, then the project possesses a business profile but remains dormant until a provider is required. This then triggers the established processes of buyer procurement, vendor selling, and contracting. This section illustrates some of the difficulties encountered.

Procurement

When the project has a profile, a decision is made to either continue with the in-house provider or contract for a vendor. If the latter option is chosen, then the project enters a procurement stage summarized in Figure 7.1, and the owner becomes a prospective client.

DOI: 10.4324/9781003370031-8

Table 7.1

Contrasting attributes of in-house vs. vendor providers

IN-HOUSE PROJECTS	CONTRACTED PROJECTS
Project is a cost center	Project is a profit center
Owner's interest	Owner and vendor interest
Governed by management	Governed by contract
Open to collaboration	Competitive
Team is familiar	Team is unfamiliar
Simple structure	Complex structure
PM influence depends on reporting level	PM influence depends on contract

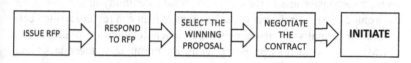

Figure 7.1 Procurement process

The client gathers requirements and distributes an RFP to the preferred list of vendor firms. There are no standards to govern this. Occasionally, a client has the budget checked by a third-party consultant who is privy to project details but forbidden from bidding. Rarely, vendor feedback will be solicited and incorporated into the issued documents. Risks can occur by failing to filter unqualified candidates, incomplete requirements, misrepresentations, and premature estimates leading to incorrect budgets.

The vendors work to prepare proposals fully compliant with requirements. Alternatives are usually disallowed. Proposal formats are often dictated by the client, but there is no standard for clients to follow. RFP clarifications may be provided, usually in open forum at a bidders' conference. Inconsistencies (e.g., need for high quality *and* rapid delivery) are seldom discussed at these meetings in order to avoid competitive disclosures or client antagonism, and are therefore unresolved. Risks arise from lack of RFP clarity, and effort wasted from discarded responses, cancelations, or withdrawals and re-issues.

Clients use a variety of techniques and processes to select a winning bid. Although there is no standard, there is usually a degree of consistency found in the marketplace (short lists, decision matrices, presentation templates, references, legal T&C boilerplate). Risks arise from prejudged preferences by clients and unwarranted assumptions by vendors.

A client's appreciation of project principles can help avoid trouble. If the client's procurement process is based on unfounded budgets, ignorance of risk and estimating disciplines, and ambiguity on quality, then they are flirting with disappointment, or worse.

Selling

For the vendor, the selling stage is the mirror image of feasibility and procurement. Project materialization boils down to hunting for opportunities, and when one is located building a bid and submitting what is hoped to be a winning proposal. These stages are the responsibility of the sales executive in whose territory the opportunity lies.

Establishing company procedures for the early stages of the sales process is a tricky issue. Understandably, salespeople regard these as a constraint on their responsiveness to the client, or on their flexibility in a competitive environment. At their discretion, sales management can require written call reports, or formal sales assessments. Customer Relationship Management (CRM) systems, such as Salesforce.com, are normalizing these tasks and are reportedly making the sales process more manageable.

At some point, if an RFP is issued, or a client's project profile is discernable, then the vendor has grounds for engagement. With this information, the vendor must decide whether to move to the bid stage. Many factors specific to the vendor's situation will play into this decision. A rational platform for the bid decision can be simple qualification checklist. This is a preamble to risk assessment in subsequent stages.

If the vendor decides the costs of bid preparation are acceptable given the win probability, proposal works begin. Two potentially conflicting objectives must be met: to prepare and submit a winning proposal, and to ensure the proposed project can be delivered. There is no standard practice for this, but five basic steps, some of which may be executed in parallel, can be contemplated: (1) plan the response to the customer's RFP, (2) do a risk assessment, (3) build the proposal response, (4) prepare the bid estimate, and (5) gain internal approvals. This level of formality allows sales and delivery management to properly engage and ensure their approvals take both objectives into account.

Contracting

The need for a contract influences the vendor's proposal work and the client's procurement. Stipulations regarding price and schedule are obvious, but terms and conditions may also be problematic. The client attempts to use the competitive environment to insist on their contractual requirements as non-negotiable, but when the preferred vendor is selected many elements remain unresolved and carry forward into initiation. They must then be negotiated before signing or, if agreement cannot be reached, the runner-up vendor is selected instead.

The separation of the business and project lifecycles means contracting for a rolling wave approach is handled very logically. There can be many contracts for one project. As the project moves through the various waves, multiple contracts are enacted, each with initiation, execution, and completion stages. But the project remains unified, proceeding through its project lifecycle. For example, the first contract might be for the requirements and design, the second for build and test, and the third for implementation.

Clients sometimes prefer to simplify the contracting and issue one RFP and one contract for the project from beginning to end. This can work well for smaller projects, but with increasing size the 'big bang' approach adds to the vendor's execution risk quite significantly. So, they usually take additional mitigating actions such as extra effort for requirements and design during the RFP response. The client cannot stay immune from this and other vendor mitigation efforts, so the resulting complications during execution can often make the rolling wave the preferred approach.

The type of contract, such as fixed price versus time and materials, influences the working relationships and the project approach. Each party will have an opinion on the best option based on the scope and inherent risk of the contract. The client should expect a fixed-price contract to include extra cost to compensate the vendor for increased risk. The vendor should understand the client may have real budget constraints and open-ended time and material costs are just not viable. There are always alternatives to these options, and they should be negotiated.

Summary of Main Failure Causes

The unproductive client and vendor interactions and inefficiencies can be summarized in the following points:

- Faulty RFP. This can be caused by lack of clear scope definition, ambiguity of requirements, incompatible demands, and inadequate commercial or technical research. Either the RFP is canceled or withdrawn and reissued, with effort wasted by all parties, or vendor responses will be inconsistent with client expectations resulting in inflated costs or a failed project.
- Vendor Selection Errors. The process may not filter unqualified candidates, may be subject to misrepresentations, may allow incorrect estimates, and may be prejudged. This is really a fundamental failure of the competitive process which completely erodes its economic effectiveness.

- Wrong Contract. The contract may be the incorrect type (e.g., time and material work being attempted under a fixed-price contract), contain inefficient terms, or exhibit complexity that excessively delays start-up.

These are concrete issues capable of being directly addressed, but there are many indirect insidious risks which can accumulate and create an escalated threat.

Owners often contract projects in the belief they are transferring risk to the vendor. This is only true in the financial sense and is usually limited. In fact, project outsourcing introduces brand new causes of failure, and traditional causes can be intensified. Table 7.2 shows some of the causes of risks and errors engendered in contracted projects during materialization. They can be mitigated during this stage, so the losses they cause can be reduced.

Obviously, many negative procurement events cannot be avoided and 'come with the territory'. Bids can be canceled, scope can change, pricing can be challenged, and schedule needs are often important. But if all parties can be transparent about the factors in play, there is a much better chance of the client getting what is wanted. And if things don't work out, then vendors are left with the knowledge their efforts were valid and not wasted.

Merits of Collaboration

This brings us to the merits of collaboration during the early stages of project materialization.

Paradoxically, although skeptical clients might feel otherwise, benefits could accrue as much to clients as to vendors if a collaborative approach is

Table 7.2

Listing of Ancillary Failure Causes

Unrealistic expectations	Commercial pressure
Different perspectives	Inadequate resources
Hidden agenda	Miscommunication
Vendor arrogance	Ignored risks
Marketplace free for all	Political over-rides
Over-optimism	Bad experiences
Over-selling	Unexplored assumptions
Lack of priorities	Over-controlling
Lack of specificity, ambiguity	Inattention to responsibilities
Playing the vendor field	Surprise requirements
Inadequate client funding	Unsupportive policies
Lack of client consensus	Sponsor inaccessibility
Missing commitments	Immaturity
Inappropriate contracts	

adopted. I have witnessed considerable client effort spent on failed tenders, or contracted projects that failed to deliver. Collaboration can also alleviate the over-dependence on the vendor which can be both costly and risk prone. Clients tend not to properly examine methods used by their vendor, often fail to ask for meaningful status, fail to train their own staff, totally delegate the vendor to deal with risk and quality, and often by default let the vendor PM drive the project.

Surely a main reason for the litany of problems with the classic procurement process just reviewed is the lack of collaboration as a procedural criterion. Interfaces between the parties occur primarily at the beginning and at the end of each stage. They are typically formal and restricted, and characterized by inadequate information flows. This, vendors claim, prevents them from doing their best job. The question is, could they be welded into two joint stages and still preserve a competitive environment?

As I hope I have shown, there are some excellent reasons to try and achieve this.

A Collaborative Commercial Lifecycle

The idea of collaboration in procurement is not new. The concept of 'just-in-time' supply management and inventory reduction could not have been achieved and become standard in many industries without customer and supplier collaboration. The CPFR model (Collaborative Planning Forecasting and Replenishment) is an ambitious extension into a multi-vendor environment which has met with some success. These initiatives are intended primarily for the manufacturing world, and the unique issues of professional services procurement remain to be satisfactorily addressed. The challenge is to offer collaboration at the front end where scope, estimates, risk, and quality might be uncertain or ambiguous, while at the same time maintaining a fair and competitive environment.

Despite the case for a joint lifecycle during materialization, there will be nagging concerns about protecting the client's confidentiality and maintaining the advantages of a competitive response from vendors. Clients should abandon the idea all risks and problems are delegated to the vendor. Adopting this perspective emphasizes projects are always a joint endeavor and helps point the way to collaboration.

Some further restrictions and requirements need to be observed:

Attributes of Collaborative Project Materialization

- Formalization. The commercial sensitivities of joint working during this front-end stage require signed agreements on information handling, working methods, and confidentiality.

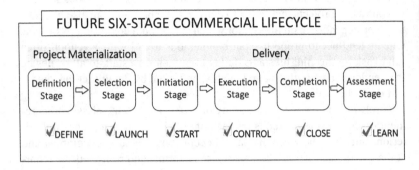

Figure 7.2 Future six-stage commercial lifecycle

- **Common Sense.** Joint activities should make sense to both buyer and seller without attempting to subsume internal or confidential activities.
- **Business.** The theme must be business efficiency and convergence of business interests by both parties.
- **Flexibility.** Multiple paths should be available based primarily on complexity criteria.
- **Generality.** Methods should be implementable at a generalized level without the need for detailed procedures.
- **Documentation.** There should be minimal requirement for new documents, consistent with clarity and need for management records.
- **Elements and Practices.** The concept of DO elements can be applied to the materialization stage, and existing practices extended as needed.

The business lifecycle is now expanded into the Commercial Lifecycle in Figure 7.2, especially for the client/vendor engagement. These two added stages are now described, emphasizing the points of collaboration designed to ensure a level playing field and improve efficiency.

Define the Project

Collaboration is important at this early stage, but jointly approved documents are unrealistic, and few are expected. The revolutionary characteristic of this stage is the early involvement of vendors and their anticipated role in shaping the project. This joint activity provides the client with an early opportunity to informally evaluate suitability of vendors and adjust screening criteria. It also allows vendors to amend their suggestions and proposals as they become familiar with the client.

The goal for the client is to create a blueprint of the project and its finances, and the goal for the vendor is to draft a working decision on bid/no bid.

The stage formally starts with the issue of a Request for Expression of Interest (RFEI) to vendors in the marketplace deemed by the client to be competitive. Vendors are asked to substantiate their interest with an account of their suitability and relevant competencies. For larger projects, meeting the objectives of this stage must be allocated in a reasonable timeframe. A preliminary scope must be assembled, technology decisions made, and sufficient data collected to prepare a cost/benefit for the feasibility study. Links to the client's strategic plan are established and budgetary forecasts are prepared.

The path followed by the vendor is driven by the sales executive because this is marketing stage, despite the need to engage technical specialists. Management applies disciplines such as call reports, win probability, CRM inputs, and an estimate of bid costs to feed into the formal bid/no-bid decision pending receipt of the RFP.

The stage exits when a preliminary project scope is defined, and a list of competitive vendors is compiled who are willing to bid given the expected requirements in the RFP.

The following are specified as collaborative Definition Stage elements and practices:

(1) Scope Delineation. A review forum is scheduled to discuss and comment on the client's current view of project objectives, functionality needs, wants, and nice-to-have, and the implied scope of work. Suggestions and alternatives from the vendor community are expected.

(2) Technology Options. A review forum is scheduled to discuss and comment on the client's current view of the technology platform and technology elements in the architecture. Suggestions and alternatives from the vendor community are expected.

(3) Risk Management. To ensure respondents have a reasonably consistent view of the project risk, the practice is extended, adding an early analysis and review forum. An example of factors might include anticipated size and duration of contract, type of contract demanded, strength of the client relationship, understanding of scope, the vendor's experience with the solution, and access to the required skills.

(4) Quality Management. To ensure respondents have a reasonably consistent view of the project quality required, the practice is extended with an early analysis. A review forum is scheduled, and grade of quality is used as a framework with various criteria assessed to determine whether a basic, standard, or superior grade is required.

(5) Estimate Counselling. A new practice is envisaged for project materialization. During definition and following sufficient work on scope and technology options, the client reviews the basis for budget estimates with interested vendors. Vendors can be invited to provide their own

confidential ballpark budgetary estimates, and the client can provide data known to affect the estimate without compromising competition. Currently, isolating the client's budget from the vendor's estimate in the cause of competition works against the attainment of a viable and successful project. The review also includes a discussion of potential functional or scope options to be included in the RFP to promote a competitive response, in addition to normal competitive pricing.

Select the Vendor

Following the Definition Stage, the client has a file of useful material to be crafted into an RFP which should now be familiar to the vendors, though this remains purely a client document. Its content and terms are the client's. The publication of the RFP initiates the selection process.

The goal of the Selection Stage is to identify a preferred vendor and a runner-up. The goal of the vendor is to win the bid with a proposal for a deliverable system.

The RFP is circulated to vendors who responded to the RFEI, confirmed an intent to bid, and who meet the client's screening criteria. Those who did not meet the client's screening criteria are sent a notice. The longlisted vendors, who have formally committed to bid, now prepare and submit their proposals and responses to required contractual terms for client evaluation. They then wait to be shortlisted, in which event they are invited to an individual meeting and Q&A session.

The vendor path concentrates on developing an estimated, compliant solution, preparing the proposal, assessing and mitigating risk, and completing their own internal review and approval procedures. This involves not just the sales executive but also the delivery manager who must sign off on the proposed system's deliverability.

The stage exits when a vendor is selected who is willing to enter contract negotiations. The following are specified as collaborative Selection Stage elements and practices:

(1) Notice of Bid Screening. Not strictly a collaborative process, it is important to include as it makes the selection process more efficient for both vendor community and the client. It improves the productivity of the selection stage. Vendors who attended the forums (which is a screening criterion) and expressed an intent to bid, but failed other screening criteria, are sent the results of the checklist and offered a review meeting. At this meeting the vendor may submit information to refute the screening results, in which case the vendor may be presented with the RFP. This is the client's decision.

(2) Risk and Quality Management. These practices require a coherent expression of need in the RFP and a response in the proposal. The vendor contribution to the collaborative forums during definition is evaluated as well as the completeness of their response. Both contribute to the overall decision criteria for vendor selection.

(3) Estimate Counselling. The Estimate Counselling practice is the strongest feature of collaboration during this stage, by far the most useful, the most innovative, and the most controversial. At this stage, the practice is focused on creating a common understanding of the basis for the vendor estimates, while at the same time maintaining a competitive environment. The principle governing this practice is to discover and share all the elements that affect the estimate equally between all responses, without compromising the benefit of vendor insights and estimating skills used to create a superior bid.

One essential technique introduced into Estimate Counselling is wedge issue elimination. A wedge issue drives the client and the vendor further apart for no good reason, and to the detriment of getting a good proposal. A mutual understanding of the requirements and project environment naturally generates a convergence of budget and estimate, whereas wedge issues lead to divergence. Table 7.3 shows a list of common wedge issues and the best practice to eliminate them.

Prerequisites to Collaboration

The reader might now be thinking the level of collaboration I have just described is so far removed from present reality as to be unrealistic. Nonetheless, I hope the benefits of adopting these practices convince both vendors and clients to contemplate the possibilities. The key question is – what are the prerequisites for such a reality to come to pass? There are two, I believe.

(1) Trust. A major challenge to the collaborative approach is abandoning the silo mentality and the reluctance to share information. In the process of working together, both parties must be comfortable sharing information. Simply put, people must trust each other.
Trust is a crucial ingredient for building commercial relationships and is always conditional, difficult to establish, and can easily dissolve. Without trust, work can still proceed, but what is already hard becomes harder.

Table 7.3

Best Practice for Wedge Issue Elimination

WEDGE ISSUE	BEST PRACTICE
Ambiguity	The client should strive to remove ambiguity from their requirements, and vendors should not hesitate to question if it is encountered during the Definition Stage forums
Conflation of Estimate and Price	These are two different data. An estimate is expressed in work-hrs, and then it is priced. The parties should not argue about one, when they mean the other
Pending Decisions Which Affect the Estimate	The client makes these decisions before releasing the RFP
Wrong Contract Type	The collaborative Definition forums would have identified contracting methods to suit the nature of the project and the needs of the client and the vendor
Avoiding Assumptions	Assumptions are essential to a realistic estimate. For example, an unmade decision must be covered by an assumption. Vendors are entitled to make whatever assumptions their estimators require, revealed only to the client in their proposals, but the client makes known to all vendors those assumptions expected to affect all estimates
Ignoring Risk and Disguising Contingency	Known risks are shared with all vendors, and proposals are evaluated on their response. Allocated contingency amounts are explicitly quoted in proposals, as are contingency plans
Specifying an Unreasonable Approach	The collaborative Definition forums would have identified acceptable approaches to the project

Common social guidelines contributing to trust building can be applied to the DO:

How to Build Trust

- Understand the difference between making a commitment and a promise.
- Don't overpromise.
- If a promise is not going to be kept, advise ASAP and apologize; keep the next one.
- Never tell tales behind someone's back.
- Don't disparage the competition.
- Don't claim credit if it isn't yours.
- Don't tell secrets; have confidential conversations but keep them confidential.

- Tell the truth and differentiate truth from opinion.
- Build team confidence but don't gild the lily.
- If you ask a question, be sincere and pay attention to the answer.
- By all means do deals and favors, but not to anyone's disadvantage.
- If you are asked explicitly for information, then provide it.
- If asked for confidential information, well, now it's complicated but you should act with integrity.

Progressively accepting commitments and responsibilities and then delivering on them will earn trust. In the final analysis, trust is demonstrated by actions not promised by words.

(2) A Trustee Role. Locally, where larger clients and a handful of vendors are well known to each other, trust may be sufficient for the multilateral adoption of collaborative procurement and DO implementation. Using the full commercial lifecycle might be feasible in the specific circumstance of a large intensive project involving known partners. But to become widespread, it must involve a sufficient mass of vendors and buyers to maintain a competitive environment and be durable enough to make the investment in a new commercial process worthwhile. In short, it needs to be institutionalized. Realistically, this can only be achieved by the sponsorship of a professional third party who, in return for a subscription, registers clients and vendors committed to the DO and adjudicates any disputes. This trustee could provide materials, updates, and training. The obvious candidates for such a role would be one of the professional services or procurement standards organizations.

Intuitively, it seems evident collaborative methods for clients and vendors would not only improve local procurement efficiency but also properly institutionalized could produce measurable gains in national productivity. Projects will be sourced and delivered quicker, work on unfit opportunities will be eliminated, work will be estimated more accurately, and the right vendor will be chosen more often. And as a dividend, perhaps the personal benefits of working as part of a genuine team will improve job satisfaction for everyone.

References

Listed alphabetically by author:

Hornby, Robin. 2017. *Commercial Project Management: A Guide to Selling and Delivering Professional Services*, Routledge.

In tackling this neglected aspect of project management, Hornby takes the perspective of the professional services vendor whose job is to sell and deliver a project to a satisfied client and make a profit. Basing his detailed prescriptions around a vendor business lifecycle, the book describes the six essential practices the vendor must adopt. It offers practical guidance, a wealth of explanatory illustrations, useful techniques, proven checklists, real-life examples, and case stories. Beyond project management, the book also proposes a comprehensive template for building a firm whose business is delivering projects.

Hornby, Robin. 2019. *Commercial Delivery Methodology*, Google Books ebook.

The CDM is a methodology to help professional services firms formalize their business management of larger, higher risk projects. Each chapter presents a stage of the business lifecycle using a procedural format and incorporating 39 templates, 5 deployment charts, 5 process diagrams, and 17 IPOs. This unique text provides complete support for evaluation of the methodology and implementation.

Kerzner, Harold. 2009. *Project Management: A Systems Approach to Planning, Scheduling, and Controlling*, Tenth Edition, John Wiley & Sons Inc.

This classic text is periodically updated and acts as a reference to explain any detail. If I am checking my project management facts, Kerzner is my first port of call. It's all there.

Merrill, David W. and Reid, Roger H. 1981. *Personal Styles & Effective Performance*, Chilton Book Company.

One of the earliest of the several analyses based on the Myers-Briggs Type Indicator, and perhaps the most useful for project work.

PMI®. 2013. *A Guide to the Project Management Body of Knowledge (PMBOK® Guide)*, Fifth Edition, Project Management Institute, Inc.

The PMBOK® has become an industry standard in North America. It is based upon a detailed, theoretical analysis of the 47 or so processes and the many more techniques seen to comprise the work of the project manager.

Thorp, John. 1999. *The Information Paradox: Realizing the Business Benefits of Information Technology*, McGraw-Hill.

Unfortunately, the paradox still remains, though thanks to John Thorp's ground-breaking analysis of business benefit methodology, there is much better awareness of what needs to be done.

Verma, Vijay K. 1995. *Human Resource Skills for the Project Manager*, Project Management Institute, Inc.

A comprehensive account of the 'soft' skills of most benefit to the project manager.

PMBOK®, PMI®, and PMP® Are the Registered Trademarks of the Project Management Institute. PRINCE2® is the Registered Trademark of OGC.

Glossary

Explanation of abbreviations and special terminology used in the guide.

Baseline   Values of the triple constraint set in the approved project plan which can only be changed by an approved change request.

Business Lifecycle   In a project context, refers to the stages of project materialization and delivery used to exercise owner control of the project.

CIO   Chief Information Officer.

Client   Specific term for the owner of a contracted project.

Commercial Lifecycle   A proposed extension of the business lifecycle providing for a shared, collaborative approach by owner and vendor(s).

CPFR   Collaborative Planning Forecasting and Replenishment.

CR   Change Request.

CRM   Customer Relationship Management.

Delivery Organization   A collective term for both the owner and provider who have adopted the themes of collaboration and business management of projects and are working together.

DM   Delivery Management or Delivery Manager.

DO   Delivery Organization.

DO Elements   Documents, techniques, or methods referenced from DO1 to DO22. There are ten categorized as core and 12 as required. They form the backbone of the Delivery Organization.

DOC   Delivery Organization Curator.

ETC   Estimate to Complete.

FP   Fixed-price contract.

Grade   An aspect of quality which allows variation (e.g., basic, standard, superior) in the rating of quality factors, to align with the owner's purpose.

In-house provider   Specific term for a provider from the owner organization.

IPO   Input, Process, Output usually represented on a methodology chart.

ISO9000 An International Standards Organization specification for quality management requiring organizational registration and inspection to certify their processes.

IT Information Technology.

Lean An imprecise term used in this context to suggest minimalist use of project management process with the intent to improve agility and reduce cost.

Lifecycle mapping A technique using the project lifecycle framework to allocate PM activities (or deliverables) to each phase, identify them as POCL, and assign them to a project manager.

Matrix Management A common method of management that superimposes a project reporting structure on an established functional organization.

MTBF Mean Time Between Failure.

Owner Generic term for the beneficiary of the project.

PARIS Coding for the RAM: Participate, Accountable, Review, Input, and Sign-off.

Performance Chain Conceptual links between a declared objective and project work which denote specific measurable threats to achievement.

Phase A cohesive part of a project lifecycle comprising activities designed to create related deliverables that meet the phase objective.

PIP Personal Improvement Program.

PM Project Management or Project Manager.

PMBOK® Project Management Body of Knowledge published by the Project Management Institute.

PMO Project Management Office.

POCL Plan, Organize, Control, and Lead are the four functions of project management.

PPT People, Process, and Technology are the contributors to the quality of activities.

PRINCE2® Projects in a Controlled Environment version 2 provides another view of the organization of project management and has become a well-known methodology in Europe, particularly in government institutions.

Product Quality The degree to which the quality factors which serve objectives are incorporated into the product.

Project Class Projects of the same type, developing comparable deliverables, operating in a consistent application area, using the same methodology, and with similar attributes,

Project Lifecycle A sequence of defined phases producing deliverables to progressively meet the project objectives.

Project Materialization   A set of processes executed by the owner and secondarily the provider to establish a project with a defined profile prior to initiation.

Project Model   A representation of the core components of a project and their interrelationships.

Project Quality   The degree to which activities efficiently create the product quality factors.

Prologue   An informal term for requirements and feasibility work that precedes project initiation.

Provider   Generic term for the manager and executor of the project work.

QA/QC   Quality Assurance/Quality Control

QMS   Quality Management System.

Quality Factor   A describable, tangible component or attribute of a product which contributes to product quality.

Quality Models   Representations or analogies usefully applied to components of the project model to create quality.

RAA   Responsibility, Accountability, Authority.

RAM   Responsibility Assignment Matrix.

RFEI   Request for Expression of Interest.

RFP   Request for Proposal.

Risk Alert   A measurable condition during project execution indicating risk level as red, yellow, or green.

Risk Event   A predicted event expected to negatively impact the project.

Risk Facet   An entity in the project environment whose associated features or conditions can act as a source or catalyst for risk.

Risk Factor   A specific feature or condition of a risk facet.

Risk Portfolio   A collection of projects managed by senior management to align with an established level of aggregate risk.

Risk Rank   A quantitative assessment of project risk based on the aggregate value of risk factors identified during project planning.

ROI   Return on Investment.

Rolling Wave   A project execution concept that imagines work focused on achieving a succession of deliverables, each driving the project further to completion. If each wave is managed as a separate contract, this is in contrast to a 'big bang' contract.

ROT   Rule of Thumb.

RYG   Red, Yellow, and Green used as a standard alert signal.

Six Sigma   A quality management system to control the results of processes within defined statistical limits.

SOP   Standard Operating Procedures.

SOR   Statement of Role.

SOW   Statement of Work, also Scope of Work (synonymous).

Stakeholder   An individual who may be a provider, an owner, or a third party with an identifiable interest in the project and a corresponding responsibility.

Success Factor   An activity, attribute, or condition judged very influential for project success.

T&C   Terms and Conditions in a contract.

T&M   Time and Materials contract.

TOC   Table of Contents.

TQM   Total Quality Management.

Triple Constraint   Time, cost, and scope. This is the current convention and used in this book though historically time, cost, and quality were also used.

Vendor   Specific term for a contracted provider.

VMO   Value Management Office.

Waterfall Lifecycle   A type of project lifecycle with each phase required to complete prior to starting the next. An exception to this rule is the technique of fast tracking which allows phases to overlap.

About the Author

Robin Hornby worked in Information Technology for over 40 years, taught project management at Mount Royal University for 12 years, and maintained a consulting practice. He pioneered many of the delivery practices described in this guide. He is now semi-retired, continues to write, and occasionally facilitates learning events.

Following his degree in Aeronautical Engineering, Robin's career began in the United Kingdom as a systems engineer with a major computer vendor. Moving to Canada in 1977, he worked for a few years in the telecommunications sector before joining an international IT consulting firm and embarking on his project management career, rising to become regional delivery manager. He later took up the position of national delivery manager for the Canadian division of a major US software vendor. Robin set up his own consulting company in 1997 and has enjoyed a variety of senior project engagements in the time since. Based out of Calgary, Alberta, Robin has experience across Canada and internationally in the United States, and the United Kingdom, Europe, Australia, New Zealand, and Hong Kong. He was a long-time member of the Project Management Institute, held their PMP designation, and presented frequently at their annual symposia.

Robin is also the author of three other titles:

Commercial Project Management – A Guide for Selling and Delivering Professional Services published by Routledge. The website is www. routledge.com/Commercial-Project-Management-A-Guide-for-Selling-and-Delivering-Professional/Hornby/p/book/9781138237681

Commercial Delivery Methodology is published by Google Play Books. The website is www.google.ca/books/edition/Commercial_Delivery_Methodology/Rbu9DwAAQBAJ?hl=en&gbpv=0

Ten Commandments of Project Management is published by TMI. The website is www.tmipm.com/books

The author may be contacted by e-mail at rchornby@shaw.ca or by phone at (403) 686–2155 for current information about Robin's availability.

The TMI legacy website is at: www.tmipm.com

Index

Printed in the United States
by Baker & Taylor Publisher Services